John H. Paynter

Joining the Navy

Abroad with Uncle Sam

John H. Paynter

Joining the Navy
Abroad with Uncle Sam

ISBN/EAN: 9783743372948

Manufactured in Europe, USA, Canada, Australia, Japa

Cover: Foto ©ninafisch / pixelio.de

Manufactured and distributed by brebook publishing software (www.brebook.com)

John H. Paynter

Joining the Navy

JOINING THE NAVY

OR

Abroad with Uncle Sam

By JNO. H. PAYNTER

Illustrated

HARTFORD, CONN.
AMERICAN PUBLISHING COMPANY
1895

Copyright 1895, by JNO. H. PAYNTER
(All rights reserved)

Dedication.

TO THE HUMAN FAMILY, WHO, THOUGH WIDELY SCATTERED AND OF MANY BRANCHES, MAY BE TRACED TO THE SAME STEM, AND, WHETHER YELLOW OR RED, BLACK OR WHITE, WHETHER WARMED BY THE GENIAL RAYS OF A TROPIC SUN, OR CHILLED BY THE FROSTS OF COLDER CLIMES, STILL WEAR THE IMPRESS OF A HIGHER BEING; AND, UNDER THE FAR-REACHING AGENCIES OF GOD'S PROVIDENCE, ARE WORKING STEADILY TOWARDS UNIVERSAL PEACE AND CIVILIZATION.

PREFACE.

It is with a degree of hesitation that I have at length decided to permit the publication of impressions formed while serving as cabin-boy on America's armored vessels, *Juniata* and *Ossipee*. These facts and impressions, while recorded partly with a view to their usefulness in passing a leisure hour by the fireside in later years, were at the same time undertaken to form a needful diversion to the often dreary monotony of shipboard life.

The prominent authors of marine literature, Clark Russell, Fenimore Cooper, Dana, Melville, and others have so rounded out and beautified their creations, portraying adventures by sea, that they have been accepted and eagerly devoured by readers of every class, young and old alike; it is not our purpose to enter the lists with these great writers, and we shall feel more than repaid if our work be instrumental in leading some of the youths of our race to cultivate a desire for that broad experience which depends so much on travel and by which one is enabled, through actual comparison, to measure the stride of different civilizations along the pathway of literature, art, and science: so the author sends forth this little volume, basing his hope for a cordial reception upon the fact that it is an accurate recounting of experiences and observations in lands far distant and among peoples whose distinctly interesting and unique characteristics may only become generally known and appreciated through the medium of the writer and historian. It is eminently fitting and proper that I do here, in these prefatory remarks, render just acknowledgments to the two commanding officers whom it was my good fortune to serve, for the kind and considerate treatment always extended, which, in many instances, reduced to a minimum unavoidable hardships, multiplied the meagre pleasures of shipboard life, and made possible the somewhat comprehensive notes from which this book is written.

CONTENTS.

CHAPTER I.
Personal Notes — Enlistment — College Days — Forced to Abandon a Prospected Profession, I Again Enter the Service — First View of the *Ossipee* — A Visit to the Captain — A Farewell to College Mates, . . 13

CHAPTER II.
Roughing It — The Work of Fitting Out — Preparing to Receive the Captain — Naval Recruits — My Friend H——, ... 28

CHAPTER III.
Leaving League Island — Our First Night at Sea — Inspection and Trial Trip — An Unforeseen Occurrence — Getting Ready for Sea — "All Hands Up Anchor" — Farewell to America, ... 45

CHAPTER IV.
"Ship Ahoy!" — Sea Sickness — William and his Chinese Cook — Sunday at Sea — The Azores — The Bay and the City of Fayal — A Lively Scene — Native Life — Ancient Churches and Monasteries — From the Mountain's Side, ... 61

CHAPTER V.
The Rock of Gibraltar — Wonders of the Rock — An Impregnable Fortress — My First Visit Ashore —

Spanish Town — Domingo, the Spanish Guide — A Fete Day of Southern Spain — The Fair Grounds — A Bewildering Scene, ... 79

CHAPTER VI.
The Bull Fight, ... 93

CHAPTER VII.
A Sailor's Plight — Along the African Coast — Target Practice — Palermo from Shipboard — An Inexpensive Meal — The Cathedral — The Tomb of Kings — Within the Catacombs — The Sicilian Vespers — An Unexpected Hello! — The Captain Sees Justice Done — A Foc'sle Concert — Attractions of Messina — An Evening at the Opera — Off for Port Said — Independence Day at Sea, ... 101

CHAPTER VIII.
An Egyptian City — A Visit to the Arab Settlement — Concert Halls and Female Orchestras — A Native Arab Dance — Through the Great Suez Canal — The Red Sea — East Indian Divers — Ceylon, the Island of Palms and Spices — British Enterprise — Social Features of Colombo — Mineral Deposits and Valuable Woods, ... 123

CHAPTER IX.
"Tiffin" — A Foreigner's Views of America — The Museum of Ceylon and its Priceless Treasures — At the Shrine of Buddha — A Religious Procession — An ex-Khedive in Exile — The Native Market, . . . 151

CHAPTER X.
Singapore — Off for the Land of Flowers — A First View of Hong Kong — Business Houses — A Chinese Auc-

CONTENTS.

tion — An Old American Sailor in Business — Col. John S. Mosby, the Celebrated Guerrilla Chief, Consul at Hong Kong — Arrival at Shanghai — A Cordial Welcome from American Ships — Old-time Shanghai — The Modern City — Foreign Concessions — A Chinese Race Course — A Sad Event — Class Distinctions and Peculiarities, ... 170

CHAPTER XI.

Among the Japanese — Charming Nagasaki — A Japanese Gunboat — Homely Arts and Industries — Notable Traits of Character — Reforms in the Social System — Land and Water Population — The Native Sampan — Picturesque Costume and Head Dress, ... 193

CHAPTER XII.

Up the Min River — China at War with France — A Dreary Christmas — Within the Blockade — Missionaries from Foo Chow, ... 207

CHAPTER XIII.

The City of Foo Chow — Sight-seeing with One of the Boys — Sailors' "Rest" — My Experience with a Native Barber — A Dangerous Passage — Our Little Friend Ah Quin — Final Inspection — Poor Riley's Fall — A Reception to Shanghai's Four Hundred — A Dark Night — "Land Ahead, Sir! Dead Ahead" — A Narrow Escape — Courts-Martial — Boat Races — Adieu to China, ... 219

CHAPTER XIV.

The Smoking Crater of Krakatoa — Zanzibar — African Ladies to the Front — Traffic with the Interior — Native Bazaars — The Sultan's Palace — A Glimpse of the Interior — The Sultan's Harem, ... 243

CONTENTS.

CHAPTER XV.

The Comoro Islands — Johanna, the Gem of the Mozambique — The *Juniata's* Mission — The Sultan and Dr. Wilson — The Tenets of Mohammed — A Stormy Meeting — A Parting Gift from the Doctor — The City of Mozambique — The Portuguese Fort and Prison — African Police — The Market Place — The Coast of Madagascar — A Guard of Honor — Ashore in a Surf-boat — Dining under Difficulties — Tullear Bay — Ports Natal and Elizabeth, ... 256

CHAPTER XVI.

Rounding the Cape — Table Mountain and the Majestic Lion's Head — Cape Town — A Last Frolic on Foreign Soil — "All Hands Up Anchor for Home" — A Rousing Three Cheers — The Captain's Advice — A Glimpse of St. Helena — A Newspaper Clipping — Barbadoes — The Barbadian and American Negro, . . . 279

CHAPTER XVII.

The Homeward Stretch — Hatteras Weather — Familiar Coast Marks — Home Again — A Visit from Customs Officers — Paying Off the Crew, ... 295

ILLUSTRATIONS.

	PAGE.
PORTRAIT OF AUTHOR,	*Frontispiece*
U. S. S. "OSSIPEE,"	28
ROCK OF GIBRALTAR,	79
THE BULL FIGHT,	93
INSIDE OF A BUDDHIST TEMPLE,	157
PORTRAIT — CAPTAIN JOHN F. MCGLENSEY,	181
PORTRAITS — CARY, AH QUIN, PAYNTER,	230
PORTRAITS — SHIPMATES,	295

CHAPTER I.

PERSONAL NOTES.

I BELIEVE that the public generally desires to be informed somewhat of the personal history of the author whose work engages their attention; in deference to that impression I may say briefly that I was born at New Castle, Delaware, on the 15th of February, 1862, in the house where my paternal grandmother now lives. My father came to Washington with the elder Bayard in 1858, and shortly after met my mother, who was Catharine, the eldest daughter of John and Elizabeth Brent; after a short residence in Delaware my parents moved to Washington, my father having been given a place under the government. My mother, whom I do not remember, survived but a little while the birth of my sister, who in turn after a few brief months followed her into the angel land.

Although an extremely puny child, a great amount of vitality was hidden in my little frame, and I was safely pulled through the small-pox in its most virulent form before I had seen two years, while at the ripe age of four I trotted off regularly every day after father had started for the office, wandered hatless about the city all day, and in fact realized the common remark of "living in the street."

About this time my father, who was very much concerned lest some evil should befall me being of such tender age, was providentially directed to her who proved my dearest friend; Mrs. Mary Cover, whose widowhood had been made still more comfortless by the loss of an only son at sea, took me into her home and heart, encompassed me with the watchful care of a most tender solicitude and in time seemed to take new life from her hopes and aspirations for my future welfare. How often has she said to me while clasped to her bosom, her troubled soul giving evidence in a paroxysm of tears, "*You are all that is left to me, all that stands between me and despair.*" Scarcely realizing the force of her words or appreciating fully the depth of her feelings, I would offer some little phrase of consolation, and while beseeching her not to weep the tears would well from my eyes in responsive sympathy. From four until well in my thirteenth year this good woman supplied at all points the place of mother to me, counseling, directing, punishing, rewarding; striving earnestly to the end that I should develop right principles and take a worthy place in life. At that time, my father having married again, I was taken from my home to live with him. I had hoped that my ever dear foster-mother might have lived; and that it should have been my happiness to lighten the shadows of her declining years with the ministrations of affectionate duty. It was not to be; faithful in all things, but a short while since she lay her life's burden down and her spirit was taken into the keeping of Him who gave it.

The change of home did not effect an interruption

of my attendance upon school and the regular grades were passed, until when in my sixteenth year and on the eve of promotion to the last term in the high school I was compelled to drop out on account of a partial failure of sight.

During this time I was placed under the care of the eminent specialist, Dr. William V. Marmion, and so successful was his treatment that before the year had elapsed my sight was almost completely restored. In this interim of enforced leisure was derived my first naval experience; I enlisted as cabin-boy on the receiving ship *Dale* at the Washington Navy Yard and my occasional unwitting falling off from discipline brought upon me so many hardships in the way of punishment that the probability of my ever entertaining the idea of entering this branch of service again would have been considered, at best, extremely doubtful. On one occasion, having obtained permission from the captain, J. D. Graham, to go ashore, I left the ship at four o'clock in the afternoon and should have been back at ten P. M. The hours passed all too quickly and at 11.30 I made my appearance, being an hour and a half overdue. The vessel was enveloped in the quiet of midnight, the captain having retired; but though he slept yet did he speak, for he had left orders with the quartermaster to put me on the seam without coat or hat when I returned aboard, for as long a time as I had violated my liberty; the month being February, my readers may have a faint idea of the rather chilly character of my thoughts at that time.

A few evenings after this occurrence I again found

myself in trouble; the captain had his family aboard and the smaller children slept in the forward cabin below deck. It was my duty to have the fire lighted here by 4.30; instead of turning out when called, I embraced my hammock still more closely and sweetly dreamed till nearly six o'clock. I was reported for having rendered the little ones liable to a severe cold, and after a sharp lecture at the "Mast" was sentenced to five days in the "Brig" on bread and water; through the kindness of the cook, however, I was not left entirely on this simple diet, and at least once a day I found coffee instead of water in my cup and snugly imbedded in the middle of a loaf of bread a huge chunk of butter, to which contraband comfort may be accredited whatever of fortitude I may have shown during those days of confinement. Such adverse experiences sufficed to make my acquaintance with Uncle Sam's navy a very brief one, and at the end of five weeks I had secured my discharge.

At the instance of a relative who was an alumnus of Lincoln University I entered the Freshman class of that institution in the fall of 1879, and after four years of study was graduated with the class of '83; I had, as I suppose most students do, pictured a future for myself in which great things were to be accomplished; but very few months had elapsed ere I realized that what I should in all likelihood accomplish would be in many respects vastly different from what had been forecasted in my college days; as a rule, this usually happy period of life with its sum of pleasures and pain, successes and failures, and a lively zest of rival ambitions, may be regarded as a slice of time distinct unto itself, upon which the mind will delight to turn in future years and which will afford a never-failing source of pleasurable reminiscence.

The conditions upon which colored boys attend college, except in extremely rare instances, are such that of necessity a degree of labor must go hand in hand with their education, and in this way the scant, though willing, contribution of relatives and friends to a fund of support is added to and made to carry the student along from year to year. The summer is utilized both for recuperation and profit and the future professional or business man may be seen dexterously handling the tray and napkin, or with nimble feet responding to the electric touch of fashion and luxury.

The summer of '83 was passed at Long Branch as a guest (in waiting) at one of the leading hotels, and toward the close of September I returned to Washington, happy in the prospect of being able to begin the study of medicine at Howard University, when the effect of the preceding four years of application became apparent and I was soon convinced that my eyesight would not stand the strain of a professional course; thus, compelled to abandon this, my ambition, it was during the succeeding three months, while casting about for an occupation, that an agreement was entered into between my friend, Wilson L. Cary, and myself to make a cruise in a man-of-war.

The average youth feels a desire more or less strong in early manhood to see something of the world; the little tot in the nursery, his eyes dilated with pictorial wonders and creations, sometimes natural, often imaginative; the schoolboy feeling an indistinct longing to make the knowledge of foreign parts he has acquired more certainly his own by actual experience and contact; the man of affairs awaiting the season when the garnered fruit of years of industry shall have made possible a realization of the fondly cherished dream of travel,—each and all in varying strength and degree testify to this throbbing, natural, and general impulse.

Our resolution once formed, we set to work considering ways and means, eagerly welcoming any intelligence that seemed to further our purpose. We were together several hours each day comparing notes, searching the daily papers, and occasionally making a visit to the Navy Department.

Upon seeing Cary one day during the first week of January, 1884, he showed me a clipping from the *Evening Star* of the preceding day which informed the public that Capt. John F. McGlensey, U. S. N., desired the services of a steward and cabin-boy for the cruise of the *Ossipee* in Asiatic waters; we each of us felt that the places were especially designed for us, and indeed the impression was apparently confirmed when later on that day we called upon the captain, and were, after a few brief preliminaries as to references, etc., engaged to fill these respective billets; after further talk in which our prospective duties were in a general way outlined, our interview was ended with the request that we call next morning at the Navy Department, where the orders for our enlistment would be ready.

It has been said that "uneasy rests the head that

wears the crown"; indeed how true this assertion was felt to be on that first night, when past longings and expectations were crowned with realizations, which, exerting its wizard influence, banished sleep, lengthened out the seemingly interminable hours of a winter's night and made more laggard still the lazy morn.

We were at the department early and after obtaining the order repaired to the navy yard; the ordeal of a rigid physical examination conducted by the surgeon of the receiving ship was passed successfully, and we were duly shipped as landsmen, the service designation for domestics, and for the cruise of the *Ossipee*.

The regulations governing the enlistment of men in our capacity give them the right to relinquish the service at home or in foreign waters, it being stipulated that in the latter case the government is relieved of all responsibility as regards their living and welfare. I have been informed by competent authority that this action was rendered necessary on the part of the government for its own protection, seeing that otherwise men would enter the service, designing only to get abroad, whereupon they would obtain their discharge and look to the consul or other representative for subsistence until agreeable employment was found, or failing which a passage home was expected. Regularly enlisted seamen may only be discharged in American waters.

Being under orders to immediately join our ship which was fitting out at the League Island Navy Yard, Philadelphia, our preparations, there being very little packing to do, inasmuch as we would soon exchange citizens' clothes for uniform, were soon completed, and there remained several hours in which to perform the unwelcome task of saying farewell to relatives and friends.

The news of our enlistment came as a total surprise to many, for the matter had been conceived and accomplished in less than a week, and quite a diversity of opinion regarding the wisdom of the undertaking was expressed. A dear aunt, who was one of the last to help me on with words of affection and counsel, placed an envelope in my hand and enjoining me not to inspect the contents until after the ship had sailed, said I should find in it a potent charm against shipwreck and disaster of every nature. Sometime afterwards at sea while rummaging through my effects I came across this envelope and determined to acquaint myself with that, whose mysterious power had been invoked in my behalf. It proved to be what is commonly termed a "caul," and may be described as a superfluous growth of skin about the size of the palm of one's hand and which children occasionally are said to be born with. A popular superstition prevails among most people that the child so born is endowed with more than ordinary powers of mind, and that the person who may possess it will be unusually free from the attendant ills and accidents of life.

We left Washington at 11 P. M., January 14th, a prey to mingled feelings of gladness and regret, knowing indeed that we were embarking on a perilous journey, but in no sense dismayed at the prospect, for with youth, health, and a fair intelligence, together with the inner feeling of comfort and confidence derived from our endearing friendship, we had all things to hope for and an effectual source of strength in the encounter of hardships incident to life upon the ocean.

Arriving at Philadelphia at 4.20 on the morning of the 15th we betook ourselves to Mother Miller's, whose comfortable abode for many years had been a favorite lodging place for Lincoln students when passing through or spending a holiday in the city, and were soon enjoying a pleasant though brief repose.

We were called at 9 o'clock, and, after breakfasting, started an hour later for the Navy Yard.

League Island, after which the yard at Philadelphia is named, is located at the junction of the Schuylkill and Delaware rivers and is about three miles from the center of the city. There are stages which make the trip three times a day for the accommodation of those who may have business at the yard. We happened to be too late for the first and as much too early for the second stage, and being anxious to see the ship we determined to foot the distance. The winter of '83 and '84 will be remembered as one of the severest known in this part of the country; the weather was at this time bitterly cold, snow eight to twelve inches deep covered the ground, so that a dreary tramp of more than three miles on an almost pathless road over which the wind, unhindered, swept remorsely, was at best no very pleasant prospect; but, as life's pleasures, whose fleetness we would restrain and draw them out over a greater length of time, must inevitably end, so there is compensation in the thought that human trials and vexations will also most certainly cease; and with perseverence we in due time were rewarded by arriving aboard the *Ossipee*.

We understood that our vessel was "fitting out" at the Navy Yard, and vaguely supposed by that term was meant the finishing touches were being given her, our surprise may therefore be faintly appreciated when upon crossing the gang-plank we found the main deck a hopeless muddle of cordage, spars, sections of boilers, tool-chests, and an endless etcetera of miscellaneous ship gear extremely bewildering to the uninitiated; add to this the terrific din occasioned by the use of the hammer, chisel, and saw in the hands of a hundred workmen, and one might readily believe as we, that the *Ossipee* was as yet very far from completion. Upon inquiring for the captain or some of the officers we were informed by the ship's keeper that they had not yet reported for duty, and that the captain was now staying with friends a short distance out of the city, and that we might learn his address by inquiring at the Hotel Lafayette; as the time was nearing for the hands to "knock off" we decided to wait and take advantage of the stage for our return to the city, which was a vast improvement upon our previous experience. Arriving uptown we at once set about appeasing an increasing sense of hunger, which was abundantly satisfied at a Market street restaurant, and feeling renewed in body, the question of passing the evening was answered by agreeing to attend the theatre. It was found upon consulting the amusement column of the *Evening Telegram* that for the trifling (?) outlay of one dollar the exquisite pleasure of hearing the famous (now lamented) Abbott might be ours. That pleasure *was* ours, and the memory of that evening with the great Academy of Music packed from pit to dome, the immense audience thrilled, enchanted as she rendered that soul-stirring melody, "The last rose of summer", is still fresh in mind, and was often recurred to with pleasure during our voyage.

We called at the Lafayette the next morning, and, upon learning the captain's address, went out to Clearview Mansion and found him suffering with an attack of rheumatism. He was pleased to see us, regretted the slow progress in the completion of the ship, and said that in view of the state of affairs at the Navy Yard we need not report again until the following Wednesday.

We returned to town rejoiced at having a few days additional liberty, but perplexed as to how we might pass the time and live within the limits of a very much depleted purse; the question was solved by Cary accepting my invitation to accompany me down the Delaware and spend a few days with grandmother. How sweetly tender do the thoughts of the place of our birth come to us in later years; though it be the most quiet, uneventful little village in the world, and though our later ideas and operations may have grown to fit a larger sphere, still we turn with pleasure to our native heath where associations to memory dear make us ever welcome. I had spent several summers here during public school days, the first of which was in the lifetime of my great-grandmother, who, at the age of one hundred and seven years, retained a remarkable vigor, taking daily walks about the garden supported by her stick and sublimely conscious of and happy in the thought of the change that was so soon to come to her; with these and like pleasant reminiscences my mind was busy on our journey to New Castle, and when upon arriving at the old home the folks vied one with the other in emphasizing a loving welcome, it was impossible but to appreciate the immense sacrifice of comfort and pleasure we were about to make for experience and travel.

Such thoughts were but transitory, however, and we were soon making plans for the thorough enjoyment of our holiday. My young friends with whom I had often enjoyed the pleasures of field and stream, the friendly rivalry for swimming honors in the waters of the Delaware, or a moonlight sail to one or another of the neighboring towns, were soon aware of my visit, and numerous suggestions were made looking to our entertainment; in consequence, our stay of four days was replete with pleasure, and indeed, as C—— has often said, they were days of unalloyed happiness in which no shadow of the hardships which were to come obtruded. And what ravenous appetites we had! Mealtime never came too soon, for us "the tocsin of the soul, the dinner bell," always had a merry jingle, and the tradesmen I have no doubt were at a loss to account for the appreciable increase in the size of their orders.

Our time so happily spent passed all too swiftly,

and on the eve of the day we were to report for duty we took our leave, followed by the prayerful solicitude of relatives and the best wishes of friends for a prosperous voyage.

We returned to Philadelphia feeling that we had about cast off the moorings that bound us to citizen life, and that for the space of at least three years we belonged exclusively to Uncle Sam. We were impatient in a manner to begin to realize on our investment, and it was something of a disappointment when we learned that on account of the slow progress in the work on the ship another week would elapse ere she would be in condition to receive the crew.

We went by appointment to see the captain, who said the delay was principally due to the exceptionally hard weather, but that he expected the crew would be ordered aboard in the course of a few days. As our funds were now nearly exhausted we obtained an advance from the captain to tide us over the intervening time. This was on the 24th, and I decided to spend the interval with my college friends at Lincoln; the steward, having several important matters to look after, among which was the securing of a cabin cook, felt constrained to remain in town. My visit was a most pleasant one, for, as is generally known, there is a sort of freemasonry about college life which makes all, in different degrees, perhaps, share the achievements as well as misfortunes of the common brotherhood. My proposed voyage was soon generally known, and in consequence, the halo of romance enveloping me, I became a most important individual. My stay included Friday, on which evening the literary societies assembled. I had during my college course been an active adherent of Garnet Lyceum, and on this evening, by unanimous vote, the order of exercises was waived and I was invited to address the association; a number of my classmates who had returned to the university and were taking a course in theology were present, and at the close of the meeting something of a love feast was held, which was finally adjourned or merged into a secret session in the room of Mr. S——, where, with a few choice spirits and in the enjoyment of a comfortable smoke, we recalled in happy converse many interesting events of the preceding four years.

When paying my respects to the Faculty at the close of my visit I was the recipient of much good advice, the lamented Dr. Cattell presented me with several books, and our much loved president, Dr. I. N. Rendall, in the course of his remarks, expressed with much feeling, said that while he recognized in some degree the rough character of the men with whom my work would lie, he hoped I would endeavor to exercise a missionary's influence, and so, though exerting myself along an unusual line, I would be enabled through the virtue of my action to extract much of pleasure and contentment from my position.

I was back in Philadelphia on the afternoon of the 30th, and having learned at Lincoln that Crummell, who was for some time my roommate, was living in the city and in very poor health, went directly to his home. I found him, indeed, in very poor health. Only the preceding June when I had parted from him at commencement he was apparently well and expecting to return in the fall to prosecute his studies,— but alas! the inherited and malignant seed of disease had developed with fearful rapidity and the bright, intelligent sparkle which formerly beamed through the "windows of his soul" had been replaced by a dullness which was painfully apparent in his now sunken orbs; after endeavoring to talk cheerfully with him awhile I bade poor Dave good-by, knowing full well I should never look upon his face again in life.

CHAPTER II.

PREPARATIONS.

THE *Ossipee* was put in commission on the 22d of January, and those connected with her at that time can never forget the exceptionally severe character of the surroundings in which they were placed; as has been intimated in the foregoing chapter, the condition of affairs was such that the slightest comfort for the men, upon whom the hardships more heavily bore, was not attainable. We were quartered at night on the receiving ship *St. Louis*, and, her accommodations being strained by reason of this extra complement, the berth-deck was as closely packed at night with hammocks as the proverbial sardines in a box.

The men turned out at four bells, and, after breaking the ice in the river for a wash, were piped to a breakfast at six bells of hard tack and coffee, and at eight bells the hands reported aboard the *Ossipee* for the day's work. They were divided into gangs, each in charge of a petty officer or one of their number, and the work consisted chiefly of bringing aboard ship tools, hardware, apothecaries' and other stores, and, in fact, every conceivable article that might be useful for purposes of navigation or in nautical emergencies. Time is told aboard ship by bells,

THE OSSIPEE.

the number of soundings indicating the hours and half hours, thus one bell is for half-past twelve, two bells for one o'clock, and so on, increasing one for each half hour until eight are struck, when they begin again. After depositing each load the trip was wound up about the galley fire, where, for a few moments, the men would endeavor to warm their numbed and aching extremities. At eight bells the crew knocked off and went to their midday meal, the chief luxury of which was vegetable water, sometimes called soup. At such a time there was usually a friendly scramble for pans, cups, and spoons, and here, as elsewhere, the force of the saying, "First come, first served," was unwritten law and rigidly observed. The messes being abnormally increased, those who were left on the ragged edge, after the necessary equipment had been procured, would receive their supply and hie themselves away to the most convenient spot, where they could more comfortably swallow their ammunition. It never takes Jack long to dispatch his food, which would seem to promise a very high rate of dyspepsia and accompanying ills, but experience fully disproves this idea, and a more healthy set of men in this particular cannot be found. One very natural reason which may account for speed in this operation is, that the shorter the time so spent, the greater the period left for recreation, and, to a sailor, a meal is but half a meal without a smoke afterwards.

At two bells the work of the morning was resumed, and continued till eight bells, when, on account of the shortness of midwinter days, all work was knocked off for the night. Supper was served at two bells, and from then until eight bells was enjoyed a relaxation from discipline and the hardships of the day, the smoking lamp, which may be regarded as the symbol of shipboard recreation, remaining lighted during the interval.

The leisure evening hours were passed in various ways as inclination suggested, spinning yarns, dancing, singing, boxing, and games of dominoes and checkers being the most usual forms of diversion, and these were entered into with much zest; a good joke would be passed along with a hearty laugh from one to another; the waltz, the favorite dance aboard ship, had also many devotees, and to the sweet strains of the accordeon, the usual accompaniment, the boys would caper with an abandon of grace truly amusing, and which was always witnessed with pleasure by the more sedate. Here, as is the case at dancing schools or public entertainments, the best dancers always choose their partners from their own class, leaving the inexperienced to hop and jump about as best they may.

In this way the discomforts of the day were tempered and rendered more endurable through the innocent pleasures of the evening, so that when "pipe-down" was sounded at eight bells by the boatswain's mate, admonishing all hands to refrain from loud talking and to suppress unseemly noises, candles were snuffed and we "turned in" to seek in our hammocks peaceful sleep and immunity from care until the coming of another day.

On the 4th of February the work upon our ship was considered sufficiently advanced for the accommodation of the crew, and accordingly the restricted quarters aboard the *St. Louis* were abandoned without regret for the more roomy and in every way superior conveniences of the *Ossipee*. Still she was in no sense completed, but it seems that the department, wearying of the long delay, had ordered that she be taken possession of by officers and crew and that ship routine be as soon as possible inaugurated.

On the 5th the steward received instructions from the captain, who was visiting his family at Washington, to have the cabin in order for his reception, as well as dinner, on the following Saturday.

The captain's quarters at this time may be described as a scene of the most elegant disorder, the various requisites of furniture, furnishings, silver, glass, and chinaware, which in generous proportion are allowed by the Bureau of Equipment for the use of the commanding officer, were scattered about the cabin deck in a tangle of confusion. With the assistance of several "hands" detailed for the purpose and strict application, good progress was made in bringing order out of chaos, so that by Thursday evening the cabin was in readiness except in some few final details which waited upon the captain's pleasure.

The steward had so far given himself no concern in the matter of securing a cook, as he understood the man who had served in that capacity on a former cruise with the captain desired to go again. It was, therefore, very annoying to learn at so late an hour that he had declined going, and that he, the steward, was expected to engage a man for that billet.

To obtain a good cook is ordinarily a rather difficult

matter, and on this subject the domestic economy of the average household has often been disturbed, but to secure the services of a true naval *chef*, one who understands his business and one who may be depended on to produce an elaborate *menu* from, in many cases, a sadly depleted storeroom, is indeed an onerous undertaking. In this exigency leave was granted to the steward and myself extending till Saturday for the purpose of looking up this rare article and arranging minor affairs of importance to the cabin comfort.

The principal hotels and boarding-houses of the city were canvassed, and several men were found who were willing to go for a year, but would not think of a three-years cruise. In this way several hours of Thursday night were spent tramping here and there without success.

Friday morning an early start was made in another direction. Numbering among my acquaintance several of the prominent caterers of Philadelphia (in which business quite a number of colored men have been very successful), we concluded to visit their establishments, and at one of these we learned of Louis Hemberger, and, in as short a time as hansom cab could cover the distance, were in his presence. We found him presiding over the culinary department of a large restaurant, and, after a brief conversation, believed him to be what he later on in many trying circumstances proved himself, a thorough-going, kind-hearted, and ever-to-be-depended-on Dutchman. He seemed delighted with the idea ; was twenty-two years old, and his susceptible German heart bleeding freely from a wound inflicted by Cupid's dart, directed by a

PREPARATIONS.   33

fickle little American maid, urged him to embrace with fervor any scheme that would take him from the scene of his suffering.

He said it was impossible for him to leave his employment before Saturday of the following week, and though such delay would entail double duty upon the steward, he thought it best to secure him on the principle of "a bird in hand," etc., and, accordingly, Louis was engaged and agreed to report aboard the ship on Monday, the 11th of February.

We had hoped in this matter, if not successful in securing the services of a man of the same race as ourselves, that we might be fortunate in finding a foreigner in whose soul the original and heaven-born principle of equality and fellowship might not have been crushed by the baneful and proselyting system of American caste, for in the close relationship which must of necessity exist on shipboard, and especially between steward and cook of the same mess, good feeling and mutual dependence are essential to the well-being of all concerned, and to this end we esteemed ourselves peculiarly happy, as the tone of the conversation had with Louis convinced us there need be no fear on this account.

The arrangement was also mutually agreeable from the fact that we were all of about the same age, and before parting we had in a measure forecast the horoscope of our future travels and mutually congratulated ourselves upon the rare vista of experience and profit opening before us.

As an early start had to be made next morning,

B   2*

we partook of a frugal supper and repaired to our lodgings. At 4.30 A.M., when, at this season and in such weather as now prevailed, the sombre quiet of midnight is yet far removed from the gray and gradual approach of the coming day, when the ghostly shadows thrown here and there by the fitful gleam of the electric light seemingly increase the o'erpowering gloom, and the shuffling step of the roundsman alone distracts the thoughts of the early traveler, we were in the street, with head well tucked down into our collars in the effort to retreat from the keenly biting atmosphere.

Upon reaching the market place we at once fortified ourselves with a bowl of hot coffee, and then set about procuring what we wanted from a memoranda previously made.

About 6.30 we started to catch the stage, carrying between us a large market basket (loaned by the butcher), besides various parcels. Arrived at the junction, puffing from the exertion, the stage was found to have at least five minutes' start, and, indeed, might be seen in the frosty distance steadily, but no less surely, drawing away from us.

What a predicament then was ours! We had thought on the former memorable trip to the yard the lines were thrown to us in very unpleasant places, and now, with a well-filled basket and parcels enough to do business with a delivery wagon, the same trip had to be made; there could be no putting off or waiting for the next stage, for the captain would arrive during the day, and to the question, "What hast thou prepared to appease thy commanding officer's hunger?"

an appetizing answer must be made. Pulling ourselves together, a lively start was made to the music of our shoes upon the icy roadway. Slipping, sliding, panting, halting, we had pursued the uneven tenor of our way about an half hour, when the music of hoof and wheel fell upon our ears. We dropped our load, and saw a team of horses drawing a large vehicle rapidly approaching.

Cary proposed that we improve on the Jesse James method and "hold them up" for a lift by means of persuasion, and, this failing, resort to the more eloquent pleading of the "dollar of our dads." There is a current saying in the teaching of faith that the Lord helps those who help themselves; however, the origin does not concern us, 'tis the application; and we felt it true in this case, when, upon a near approach, we recognized several of the officers of the *Ossipee*, who, in turn, seeing our dilemma, kindly offered us a place in their wagon, and I have no doubt the recording angel in placing the action to their credit made extra heavy characters and subjoined the marginal note, "they did it unto two of these, my little ones."

The remaining distance was covered in such good time that by five bells we were aboard ship and had started in on preparations for the captain's reception.

The culinary arrangements aboard a man-of-war follow the same general principles of method and precision which attain in all other portions of her extensive mechanism. It is the rule that the captain's and steerage messes shall use the starboard side of the galley range, and the wardroom, being the largest, has alone control of the port side; the three cooks of these official messes look after their own supply of fuel, and the ship's cook has a general supervision of the entire galley; it is to his care the different berth-deck cooks, of whom there is one for each mess, consign their artistic compositions when ready for the oven, and when in his unerring judgment the same are considered sufficiently cooked, they are dragged forth and the respective cooks take them in charge for serving at the proper time. A mess consists of fifteen or twenty men for whom there is a cook and caterer chosen among themselves, and always with a view to obtaining the best possible service as regards economy and mess fare; in the cook the ability to make bread is the crucial requisite, the position, too, is considered in the nature of a "plum," for it usually carries with it a ration and a half ($13.50) per month which is allowed for the service, thereby materially increasing the bank account of such an one at the end of a cruise.

In the matter of rations every service man from Admiral to boy is treated equally by Uncle Sam, all being allowed one ration ($9.30) per month.

All, too, are compelled to furnish their own bedding, which is issued by the Government and charged against the individual upon the paymaster's books.

The person who exercised the important functions of ship's cook aboard the *Ossipee* was a true specimen of the old navy "salt," who approximate time and events by their cruises and who may be depended on to ship over and over again until health fails, and they are relegated to one or another of the homes provided by the Government. Our first acquaintance with Brett, for that was the name by which he mustered, was rather of an unpleasant nature. He informed the steward he would have to bring his coal from the wharf, as there was none as yet on board. He volunteered all necessary information concerning the working of the range, cook's chest, water supply, etc., and directed us where to find the coal, which was at another part of the dock and about a quarter of a mile from the ship, wholly unprotected and entirely covered with snow and ice. We shoveled out enough of the dusky gems to last through breakfast next morning and carted it aboard in buckets. This duty we performed each day and it was the heritage of the cook upon his arrival, continuing so until the ship was coaled several weeks later.

If beginning housekeeping in strange surroundings is awkward, how much more so must it be aboard an uncompleted ship in the middle of a winter of unusual severity. This, then, was our situation, but now, as always, and in whatever circumstances of an extraordinary nature the steward found himself, he proved equal to the occasion and was in a short while thoroughly at home in the performance of his new duties.

The quickened effect to be noticed about the galley on this Saturday afternoon was also a marked feature of the operations throughout every portion of the vessel. The executive officers, now in the cabin, then on the berth-deck, with the assistance of officers and petty officers in the directing of the crew, worked earnestly to the end that a cheerful and withal a shiplike appearance might greet the captain upon his arrival.

The cabin brightly lighted by swinging and bracket lamps reflecting gaily in the surface of the finely polished wood which finished the interior, the brass door-sills of the staterooms and after-cabin rivaling the handsome plate mirrors in their extreme brightness, a serviceable carpet of rich design, *portieres* of quiet hue and graceful fold, and furniture promising rare comfort as well as durability made up a refined and cozy setting for the dinner table, which stood a charming center, attractively laid with elegant service for the first meal. In due course the captain came aboard, and, upon invitation, Mr. Newman, the executive officer, dined with him at four bells. The former had brought a vigorous appetite, and an elaborate *menu* having been prepared in honor of the occasion, the whole, from oysters on the shell to coffee, was thoroughly enjoyed and elicited the remark from the captain that if C—— proved as good a steward as he was a cook, he might congratulate himself upon having secured a prize. The forward cabin, which is also the *salle à manger*, is the principal living room, and so, the dinner over and the remains cleared away to the pantry, which is built conveniently at the entrance to the cabin on the port side, the captain and his guest lighted their cigars and made themselves comfortable for a general talk upon ship affairs. Our pantry was a very snug little affair about six feet square, and, through the perfection to which the art of ship building has been brought, leading to the almost wonderful utilization of every particle of space, was thoroughly adapted to the uses it was intended to serve. Here the steward and I took our meals. A table was improvised by pulling out two of the drawers of the dresser and placing across these the bread-board, and with the aid of camp stools we were enabled to have our meals in comparative comfort. The same also served as a writing desk and was used for these purposes throughout the cruise. Upon answering a summons to the cabin at two bells, just as "pipe down" was sounding, the captain said that I might continue using my hammock for the present, but in case the rheumatism bothered him at sea he should require me to sleep in the pantry so as to be within easy call. He then complimented the steward upon the dinner and expressed himself as very much pleased with everything, adding that he knew of nothing that should prevent our having a very pleasant cruise: some further talk over mess matters brought to a close what had been an extremely busy day.

Our life now was necessarily one of constant drudgery; the only comfort possible in the circumstances was during the hours of night when tucked in our hammocks we became oblivious to all unpleasantness; each day brought its share of new duties and experiences, and whenever practical various features of man-of-war routine were introduced, so that while our hands were constantly employed, the mind was no less so in "catching on" to the many interesting details of seamanship and naval discipline. As time wore on the progress towards completion became more apparent, and near the end of February we began to look for orders from headquarters for the trial trip and subsequent movements preparatory to sailing for our destined station.

During this time the ship's quota had been nearly filled, either by transfer from other ships or new enlistments, and among the crew, the main body of whom were Americans of Irish descent, there were numbered Englishmen, Germans, Dutch, Danes, Norwegians, Italians, and Portuguese, besides several Japanese who had shipped as servants for the wardroom and steerage messes, and a Chinese cook for the wardroom who answered to the patch-work name of Joseph Ah Fah. It will readily be seen that the student of anthropology had here a rare opportunity for study and investigation, and though perhaps there was no one aboard especially interested in such researches, yet the most indifferent might occasionally find himself instituting comparisons through which would develop much information and ofttimes innocent amusement.

There were also among them men about whom one would wonder how they came to occupy their present station, who bore the impress in their face and manner of having adorned a more elevated sphere, men with a purpose and men whose purposes through some unpropitious stroke of fortune had been prematurely shattered; there were those also who found the motive for their enlistment in the mere love of adventure, to whom the excitement of travel with accompanying experiences, often thrilling and dangerous, furnished the highest class of enjoyment.

Partaking somewhat of the attributes of the two

classes just referred to, was a young Englishman whom we will call H——. He had arrived in America in the preceding fall and had passed the interval to the time of his enlistment, which occurred about the 1st of February, in the different large cities of the East, principally in New York. He had several hundred dollars when he arrived, which was soon exhausted, and midwinter found him without funds or influential friends and too proud to appeal to relatives across the water. In sheer desperation he offered his services at the recruiting station and was enlisted as coal-heaver for the cruise of the *Ossipee*. Shortly after his coming aboard we formed quite a friendship. He was well educated, a practical machinist, and had by travel and study acquired several languages, among them French and German, which he spoke fluently, while with Spanish and Italian he was almost equally at home. During his stay aboard, which to my sincere regret was but a few months, he gave me the benefit of his lingual accomplishments in an effort to acquire the French language which I had begun under private instructions during the last term at Lincoln, and my lessons with H—— at the dinner hour or while taking a constitutional on the forecastle before seeking our hammocks were always looked forward to with interest and pleasure.

It is probably a matter of impossibility to find a crew, all of whom are noted for their intelligence, industry, sobriety, and other good qualities; and while in many vessels the great majority may be counted on as safe winners in the "liberty-list steeplechase," still there are those, often véry many, against whom odds will be given and who are sure after once leaving the "post" to leap plump into the "ditch" of disgrace or running away with the bit will go wildly regardless of regulations, and are finally led back and rated ineligible for several such future events.

Thus "Jack" may be said to make for himself a ship character, and if he should by any possible accident go astray of what would naturally be expected the greatest surprise would be shown, and the circumstance, passed promptly from one to another with varying comment, would furnish gossip for several days.

Another element without which a man-of-war's complement these later years is considered incomplete, is the naval apprentice, who is enlisted at the age of sixteen and bound to the Government with the consent of parents or guardian during minority. They are well cared for, are instructed in the ordinary branches of learning, and from their ranks are recruited the best sailors of which the service boasts. There were about fifteen of this class detailed for the *Ossipee*, and a smarter or more mischievous set of youngsters never "cleared a pennant." Among them was one colored lad, whose surname was Gordon, and who, by his intelligence and good nature, became a general favorite both "fore and aft."

Another bright little fellow who was so chubby that the long, rolling, lurching walk of the sailors appeared in him most fitting and natural was Diddy Bags, and although those dearest to him would possibly fail to recognize the youthful embodiment of their hopes under this uncommon name, still it is the one under which he achieved popularity aboard ship, and there were few who knew him by anything else. Diddy was the youngest of the gang, agile as a monkey, and the ringleader in all the mischievous surprises gotten up about deck for the benefit of the old tars. These traits, however, seemed to increase his worth in the estimation of the "old boys," and the cruise was but a few weeks old before they were all his willing slaves and protectors.

Thompson, Ellis, and McCarthy complete the list of the names I can now recall of this merry set, each of whom, with a bare exception, I have lately learned, has since won his way to success in other walks of life.

A marine guard forms a part of the company of every ship above a certain class. Their duties are chiefly of a police and military character, supplementing the strong arm of the Master-at-Arms and ship's corporal in case of disturbances, or when, as sometimes occurs, shipmates return from "liberty" exceedingly groggy, unruly, and vicious. Several of the younger and more comely of the guard are detailed for duty at the entrance to the cabin as orderly or messenger. In like manner, other important points about ship are guarded by marines who do their turn according to a schedule or watch-list prepared and looked after by the corporal of the guard. They have regular positions assigned for working ship, routine exercise, and all matters of discipline. An officer of marines having quarters in the wardroom and of course subject to the higher authority of the captain, has charge of the squad.

The ship by March 1st was considered complete and ready for service, and it was thought the builders had achieved great success in rebuilding and overhauling to such an extent as to make her practically a new vessel.

CHAPTER III.

THE START.

DURING the first week in March orders were received from the department to take on magazine stores and proceed to Norfolk, where the prescribed inspection would take place; accordingly after spending two days in taking on war or rather salute material, we got under way on the 12th of March. As may be imagined there was very little regret felt at leaving League Island; every one welcomed the change and in consequence a general and hearty exuberance of spirits animated all hands; a great many friends of the crew were down to bid *bon voyage*, who, with the naval people and several hundred workmen from the yard, were gathered on the dock, —a goodly throng who cheered and cheered again as our gallant vessel moved out into the stream.

The various craft in the river joined in a hearty send-off, tooting and whistling in varying crescendo of doubtful melody, while the crews of the smaller boats yelled themselves hoarse in shouting a cheerful good-bye.

The day was all that could be wished for an auspicious start, and as we steamed on past the city, the engines seemingly vibrating with conscious power and pouring forth volumes of thick smoke from the funnel, which curled away into the faintest streak far astern, a genuine thrill of pride and pleasure animated all hearts.

So on down the queenly Delaware past Wilmington and a little further dear old New Castle with its ancient wharf, warehouse, and dilapidated battery, to all of which I threw a mental good-bye, wondering if I should view those familiar scenes again.

The entire day was passed on the foc'sle watching the Delaware and Jersey shores; both watches were on deck, and as no sail was made while in the river there was lots of time for chumming in which different speculations were indulged, such as the probable time it would take us to reach Norfolk, the vessel's speed, capacity, length of stay, etc.

The distance between Philadelphia and where the Delaware flows into the Atlantic is about 90 miles, and, at the rate of speed we were making, would be reached sometime during the first night watch. At eight bells (noon) the starboard watch was turned to and given the first sea watch. Man-of-war's men are justly noted for their zealous watchfulness in every detail touching the ship's welfare, and this will be found as true during the closing days of a cruise (which speaks volumes for the efficiency of naval discipline) as when setting out. It cannot be expected, however, that a crew gathered from all parts of the earth and working together for the first time in actual seamanship should show as fine results as is possible later on. Allowing for all this, our men, by turning to with a cheerful good will, were soon working together in intelligent harmony, and our vessel steamed on towards the great Atlantic manned by as worthy a crew as ever trod a deck.

Shortly after midnight the gradual transition from the smooth waters of the river became apparent in the rise and fall of the vessel as she met the restless sea, while the outlines of the two coasts had become but dim black streaks punctuated by a light here and there along the shore; the night was bright, starry, and cold, and everyone not engaged below was about deck enjoying the calm beauty of our first night at sea. At eight bells the watch was changed, the lookout stationed at the cat-head and the piercing whistle of the boatswain's mate stilled all unusual noises throughout ship. The master-at-arms, or, as the sailors dub him, "Jimmy Legs," after seeing that lights were out on the berth-deck made the rounds of the steerage and ward-room and reported to the officer of the deck "lights out and all quiet below." The watch, having very little to do, there being no sail made, chatted in subdued tones in groups here and there about deck or under the foc'sle, always alert for a call to brace a yard or execute any order that might be passed from time to time. After dinner, which was served the captain at four bells, everything was made secure in the cabin in case rough weather should be encountered during the night, for, as our experience afterwards verified, it is the part of prudence (and a sailor is always prudent at least aboard ship) to be prepared against sudden changes.

The captain had the charts placed on the table in the forward cabin to be referred to by the navigator and himself in making the ship's course, and after having looked after his comfort for the night I went forward and joined the steward and H———, with whom a pleasant hour was spent in conversation before turning in.

I awoke next morning at eight bells when the early watch was called on deck, and knew by the swinging motion of the hammocks that we were rolling considerably; I did not turn out immediately, taking advantage of the latitude allowed servants to lie in a little longer, and after lashing my hammock and leaving it swinging in readiness to be carried to the nettings at six bells came on deck. The men were all sitting or moving about under the foc'sle enjoying their early coffee and hard-tack; the former, smoking hot and diffusing an inviting fragrance, serves as an eye-opener for Jack and helps him gather himself together for the work which must be done before breakfast. At one bell the boatswain's whistle sounds, the cooks disappear with their coffee buckets, cups, and other gear, and the day's operations begin. Upon going aft the orderly informed me that the captain, who did not retire till very late, was not to be called until six bells. I found upon consulting the log that we had covered 112 miles, making a general average of 7 knots per hour. At four bells the word was passed to "holy-stone decks," and immediately the necessary gear, embracing blocks of stone (with two ropes attached by means of which they are dragged fore and aft along the deck), buckets, sand, mops, and brooms, was brought up from the hold, the pumps were manned, and the work begun. Washing down decks is rather Arctic work in mid-winter, to be

THE START.

sure, but every one was anxious to present a good appearance upon arriving at Norfolk; so that, turning to with a will, the vigorous exercise soon counteracted the cold, and the work proceeded cheerfully to a finish. After the scrubbing process had been completed, squilgees and swabs were used and the decks dried down. At six bells all hammocks were brought up, at seven bells the watch below was piped to breakfast, and at eight bells the watch on deck was relieved. The crew, irrespective of watches, have each their responsibility for the condition of the brass (usually called "bright work"), and the interval between breakfast and quarters is used for brightening and polishing with oil and rag every particle of brass about deck. To the guns, the carriages of which are principally brass, much time is devoted, and between the crews of these a friendly rivalry exists as to which shall present the best appearance. The captain breakfasted at eight bells, and anticipating the call to quarters at two bells the steward and I tarried but a short while over our breakfast, and while he looked after affairs in the pantry I went about the morning work in the cabin and stateroom. In a few moments the bugler sounded all hands to quarters and officers and men were filed on deck and took their places in line according to rating, the former in the starboard and the latter in the port gangway; the master-at-arms reported "all up from below," and the captain, with sword in its scabbard, going forward on the starboard side followed by the executive officer, made the round of inspection, taking in the berth deck and returning aft along the line of sailors, who, standing at attention with clothes neatly brushed and shoes polished, saluted as he passed; the surgeon, engineer, and paymaster approached the captain, saluted and reported "all's well" in their departments, after which "pipe down" was sounded and the men dispersed. The wind having come out strong the captain ordered sail made, the executive officer took the deck, all hands were called "make sail," and on the instant every man took his station. At the order "lay aloft topmen," those stationed in that part of the ship, usually apprentices, leaped into the rigging and nimbly climbing the shrouds were soon at their posts, the yardsmen followed aloft, and at the order "lay out" distributed themselves along the yard, the running gear meanwhile being overhauled and made ready on deck and the hail "All ready forward?" being answered, "Aye, aye, Sir"! the word "let go" was given, the loosened canvas fell from the yards ready to be sheeted home, and the royal and topgallant yards were swung up and into position. The marines, servants, coal heavers, and other hands on deck manned the running gear, and with a tramp, tramp, and steady pull away, every stitch is speedily hauled taut, the men aloft at the order "lay down," descended from the rigging, the various ropes were coiled up in their proper place, and, all being snug, we bowled away on our course at a speed of nearly eleven knots. Not stopping to detain the reader, who is perhaps no less impatient than the author to leave the shores of America and make a our of observation in foreign lands, we will foregot further details of the trip to Norfolk, off which city we anchored at 9 A. M., on the 14th of March. On the 15th word came from the Department that the Inspection Board would arrive on the 20th, accompanied by the Honorable, the Secretary of the Navy; in an astonishingly short time the news had penetrated every part of the ship, and, though not unlooked for, resulted in an unwonted stir and excitement both fore and aft.

The days preceding inspection brought with them excellent weather, bright and cold, which alone was sufficient cause for quickened movements and earnest action; the ship's company was carried through each day a series of drills and manœuvres to which it was thought especial attention would be given.

There were two other naval vessels in the harbor, and at eight bells each morning, when the stars and stripes were hoisted to the main, the crews would rival each other in showing the dispatch with which the light yards were sent up and sail loosened. In these movements our boys, although the youngest crew, kept well to the front with their competitors and showed by their earnest work a becoming pride in their vessel, which is one of the strongest impulses of a sailor's nature. The great day at length had come; all hands were called at one bell and after early coffee were "turned to," an increased muscular force was expended upon the holy-stoning process, and an extra effort put forward in every particular, so that when breakfast was piped at eight bells it would have been difficult to find a more clean or ship-shape vessel in any water. The word was passed for the men to dress in clean blue, and without loss of time the black bags in which Jack stores his wardrobe were overhauled, each donned his best suit, cap, and neckerchief, and with bright faces and shining shoes were insomuch ready for the exercises which were to come. The steam launch was called away to bring off the inspection party, and at two bells all hands were piped to muster. Upon the quartermaster reporting the launch returning, the marine guard was drawn up in the starboard gangway. In a few moments the party was alongside and coming up the gang ladder, the accompanying ladies, followed by the Honorable, the Secretary of the Navy, and the members of the board, were received by the captain and the officers, the guard being brought to a "present arms" as they moved aft and into the cabin; reappearing on deck, the board, under escort of the captain and executive officer, made a tour of inspection of the ship's company and different parts of the vessel, after which the executive officer took the deck, the boatswain piped down and all hands stood ready for the active work of the various drills. The principal manœuvres were completed by noon, in all parts of which the men acquitted themselves most creditably to the satisfaction of both officers and visitors and their personal gratification.

All hands were now piped to dinner. The captain had given the steward orders to prepare luncheon for twenty, and one bell found the guests with several of the officers from the ward-room seated about the cabin board.

The wife of the Honorable Secretary occupied the place of honor at the captain's right, while the other ladies were seated here and there, forming a most pleasing chain of contrasted grace and manliness. The bright uniforms of the gentlemen, the rich though modest toilets of the ladies accentuated the simple elegance of the table, and made, of the whole, a memorable scene of beauty. The steward, faithfully seconded by Louis, the cook, had gotten up a dainty *menu*, the excellence of which was fully attested, course by course.

At two bells the hands were "turned to" and preparations made for getting under way for the trial trip, and at three bells we were headed out to sea, the visitors occupying the poop from whence every movement might be plainly observed.

The ship behaved beautifully, rolling but little, through deference possibly to her lady guests, and a run of twenty miles, for the purposes of ascertaining her tactical diameter, facility of engine work, and defects of outfit and construction, was satisfactorily completed.

Returning to our anchorage, when off Cape Henry, we were set by the ebb tide too close in; a rasping, grating sound which carried consternation to all hearts, was heard — a sensible jarring, imparting a sudden and unpleasant shock as the vessel ceased to move, and we knew we were aground; the engines were immediately reversed and various methods at the command of intelligent navigation were resorted to; but in a few moments the tide itself, which was accountable for our dilemma, came to the rescue and we were again afloat and without further mishap steamed on back to our anchorage. The steam launch was immediately called away to take the Secretary and suite ashore; a salute of guns was fired in his honor, and a busy day for all hands was brought to a close. Naturally, the incident of grounding was for some days the one absorbing topic of conversation, for the possibility of its having resulted more seriously was patent to all; the Department deemed it requisite that the ship be put on the dry dock, which being done developed no injury other than the metal on her bottom being scraped here and there where she had touched.

The question of responsibility was determined before a general court-martial, ordered to convene at the navy yard, Norfolk, Virginia, April 25, 1884, and of which Commodore William J. Truxton, U. S. N., was president, at which time was arraigned and tried the navigating officer, Lieut. William I. Moore. The charge: "Culpable negligence and inefficiency in the performance of duty," to which the accused pleaded "not guilty," was held to be proven by the court, who sentenced Mr. Moore to "one year's suspension from rank and duty and to retain his present number on the Navy Register."

Everyone felt sincere regret for the unfortunate occurrence which entailed so much of disappointment and resultant annoyances upon an officer who in the short period of his service aboard had won the respectful love and confidence of all his shipmates.

After coming off the dry dock the ship was anchored about a mile from Fort Monroe. The famous Hygeia Hotel was in the full flush of a most successful season, and each day brought us numbers of fair visitors with their escorts, who through the gallant

THE START.

courtesy of the officers were made pleased witnesses of the routine, as well as being allowed a view of Jack's method of living aboard ship. At night, after the boys had had their frolic and a calm quiet, broken only by the stroke of the bell and the watchful hail of the quartermaster, pervaded the ship, sweet strains of music tuned to the requirements of the dance would be borne to our ears across the water.

The Hygeia "hop" was in progress and within its elegant ballroom might be seen the fairest flowers borrowed for a season from fashion's garden in many states. Several of our younger officers mingled occasionally with these scenes of mirth and pleasure and were brought off in the launch, which left the wharf at midnight on her last trip.

The Captain's family had come down from Washington to spend the last few days with him and were pleasantly domiciled at the Fort. The duties of the steward, cook, and myself were accordingly very light, and ample opportunities were afforded for going ashore, but, with the exception of the steward, whose business made the trip necessary, we went but seldom. My first experience* on the Norfolk ferry, when I was told by the gateman that "the other side

---

* A second experience of similar nature was undergone by Carey and myself, when, a few years later, we left Washington to go to Currituck Sound, N. C., the Captain of the miserable little side-wheeler we took at Norfolk, informed us that we could not go into the filthy hole he termed "cabin," and we were forced to remain on the open deck for more than twelve hours, a prey to the weather, which was in no sense tropical.

of the boat was for niggers," cured me of all desire in that respect.

On Tuesday of the second week of April the Captain asked me how I would like to take a run up to Washington. I told him I should be greatly pleased, whereupon he said he did not expect "sailing orders" for several weeks and that I might have a week's leave. There was very little preparation to make; my cheese-cutter suit and cap were quite new, and although I had a citizen's suit aboard, I somehow preferred wearing the uniform, and taking with me only several changes of linen I went aboard the steamer at 5.30, and after a very pleasant trip arrived in Washington early next morning. The week passed most agreeably, and indeed the days sped all too quickly, "however much I may have borrowed a few hours from the night to lengthen them out," and when Tuesday came and I took a final farewell of father and a few dear friends I felt that I should have been better contented aboard ship. There were very few passengers on the down trip, and it was a great relief that I was not compelled to make an effort at sociability; from the deck I watched with lingering view the outlines of many familiar landmarks, and when the softly fading twilight had been lost in the shadows of night a thousand lights penetrated the gloom in silent adieu. I sat in the saloon till after midnight recalling from out the past many of memory's treasures until, remembering the active work which must follow my return to the ship, I repaired to my berth, where the few remaining hours were spent in fitful slumber. The steamer arrived at Norfolk at 7.30,

THE START. 57

and at 8 o'clock I was aboard ship. My shipmates were all glad to see me back, especially a few to whom I was the bearer of messages and letters from friends and relatives at home.

Sailing orders were now daily expected, and in consequence great activity prevailed throughout every portion of the ship.

An outbound man-of-war is completely stocked by the Naval Bureau of Equipment with every essential of wear that Jack may need during the cruise. The goods, usually of excellent quality, are scaled to be drawn at the lowest possible cost; in addition may be had tobacco, blacking and brushes, whisk-brooms, shoe laces, handkerchiefs, buttons, etc., all of which are classed as small stores, and may be drawn once a month from the paymaster. The provisions with which the ship is stocked are salt beef (better known to seamen as salt horse), salt pork, flour, tea, coffee, beans, butter, sugar, molasses, and a few articles of canned food; these are also in charge of the paymaster, and are issued by him through his yeoman and Jack of the Dust at stated times. It will be seen that no small amount of labor was required to get this large supply aboard; for nearly a week barrels and boxes of all sizes were taken on and gradually and systematically stored away in the "hold"; then came the stores of the officers' messes, which were looked after by the caterer and steward of each respectively, assisted by a number of the men detailed for the purpose.

The cabin stores which were ordered from the

well-known firm of Park & Tilford of New York arrived on the 20th and found convenient storage in the deck and transom lockers with which the cabin was generously supplied.

The *Ossipee* also received an addition to her color guard about this time heretofore numbering five. We were now made six. The caterer and members of the ward room mess had become dissatisfied with their steward, an Irish gentleman by the name of Donahue, and had shipped in his stead a gentleman of color in the person of Mr. William Cook of Norfolk, formerly ward-room steward aboard the U. S. S. *Galena*. We welcomed William most cordially, especially so upon learning that he was a "member", for it is said that "a little leaven leaveneth the whole," and until his coming the ship was entirely without any leaven.

Orders came from the Department on the 22d to sail on the 30th; we were to go by way of the Mediterranean and Suez Canal, and report to Rear Admiral John Lee Davis, on the Asiatic Station, without greater delay than necessary.

On the 25th and 26th final liberty of twenty-four hours was granted each watch, and the monthly allowance having been previously issued, Jack was in becoming shape to give a rousing farewell to America; how genuine his regret at this unraveling the ties of affection for and association with the "land of the free" may be more or less accurately judged by the determined effort with which in many instances he sought to be numbered among the missing when the ship sailed. I trust I do my shipmates no injustice; possibly the snakes which were minced to an invisible fineness in the parting cup, and which is a part of the process of mixing in the Old Dominion, were of such a vipery liveliness as to recombine within the anatomy of poor Jack, and shooting the intoxicating virus into his vitals, made him an unwitting slave; in any case, however, a muster of the liberty men of both watches disclosed unwarranted absences to the number of twenty, all of whom, except two, who "never came back," were returned by the Norfolk police, who received the reward of $10 for each, the same being charged against the individual's account.

At last the day of departure had come, the crew was turned to at one bell, and before the other ships in the harbor had begun to show signs of awakening a great deal of preliminary work had been accomplished. The fresh provisions of the different messes, the ordering of which, in consideration of their perishable nature, was delayed till the last practicable moment, were alongside at four bells, as also a supply of live poultry for the officers' messes, to be resorted to when the beef and other fresh meats should be exhausted. The men of each mess, by chipping in from their allowance, were enabled to lay in a goodly stock of fresh stuff, principally potatoes, in ship parlance "spuds," cabbage, and a round or two of fresh beef, all of which were stored in the ship's boats or in the places most convenient under the foc'sle.

At ten o'clock all was in readiness for a start, and with the last mail which was sent ashore bearing many a tender message of farewell to loved ones, was cast adrift for many a long, weary month, the last tangible means of connection with home and country;

from now on 'tis to memory we must turn for an occasional glimpse of erstwhile familiar scenes and faces and by its aid to live over and over again the pleasures, joys, and albeit sorrows of our past experience. The boatswain's call of "All hands up anchor" was immediately responded to, the windlass was manned and in a short while the anchor was in sight, the "cat" was hooked, and "all hands and the cook" laid hold of the falls, and with a steady pull she was walked up to the "cat head" to the lively notes of the fifers "Marching through Georgia." The engines began to revolve and, as the ship swung round, one of the port guns which had been loaded meanwhile was run out and a parting salute fired, which was returned by the fort and the other vessels. The crew was ordered to man the rigging for a parting cheer, so, scampering here and there and covering every inch of space as far as the cross-trees and crowding the foc'sle, they, at the word, with waving caps, sent forth three hearty rounds, which elicited a chorus of hearty responses from our companion ships; another and final hurrah! the men lay down from the rigging, and we are *en route* for foreign lands.

CHAPTER IV.
" FAR, FAR AT SEA."

BEAUTIFUL sunshine, a smooth sea and winds whose winter keenness had been lost in conflict with an early spring, were the weather conditions, on this, our first day at sea.

As from the foc'sle I scanned the long line of native coast tapering off to the southward, and which grew gradually less and less distinct, I felt indeed that our lives are conceived in mystery and that from cradle to grave we follow an unseen though ever beckoning hand which leads us on through shifting scenes to the one great end:

> Oh! River of To-morrow I uplift
>   mine eyes, and thee I follow
>   As the night
>   Wanes into morning
>   Still follow, follow,
>   Sure to meet the sun;
>   And confident that what the future yields
>   Will be the right, unless
>   Myself am wrong.

We steamed along pleasantly all the afternoon, the watch below feeling no need of rest, passed the time on deck in active restlessness, as yet not having thoroughly fallen into routine life at sea. About seven bells (half past three) " Ship Ahoy! " coming from the lookout on the cross-trees drew all hands to the foc'sle, and, straining the eye, there was first discerned a faint line of smoke a point or two off the port bow, and soon the outlines of a large steamship came in evidence. The quartermaster made her out a passenger steamer of the Inman line bound in all probability for New York. When she was nearly abreast the colors of the two vessels were dipped, an act of nautical courtesy, and we both held away on our course in opposite directions. At eight bells (eight o'clock) in the evening when the watch was changed, the lookouts stationed and the quiet of the night had settled about the ship, friend H—— joined me while enjoying a smoke on the foc'sle. He had just done his "trick" below in the coal-bunkers, and through hard work and being confined in the region of heat and dust, was in a state of physical exhaustion. He said that he was very much discouraged, that the work was far too heavy for him, and he felt to be doing an injustice to himself by remaining, subject to such hardships for a longer time than was necessary. After awhile the conversation drifted into a more pleasant channel and under the witchery of the starry night he soon recovered his wonted good humor and made me a delighted listener to accounts of many novel experiences and of opinions and observations covering a wide range of subjects. I could not but feel that he had made a mistake in enlisting in the navy, for one of such rare traits as well as technical training could scarcely fail of success through application along some more suitable line of endeavor. Before going below he said he had several useful books in his bag which were unavoidably being roughly used, and of which he would like me to take charge, adding that they would possibly be of some service to me in the study of French. On going to the cabin to see that all was snug before turning in, the captain, who was engaged in a social game of cribbage, said that I had as well begin sleeping aft; so bringing my hammock up from the berth deck and spreading it athwart the pantry deck, I was soon comfortably asleep in my new quarters.

Thursday, May 1st. There was no change in the weather until late in the afternoon, when the wind came out fair and the Captain decided to make sail. All hands were called, the canvas spread, which, filling rapidly, sent the vessel along at an increased rate of speed. I sat on the foc'sle till four bells (ten o'clock) had sounded, enjoying the intense beauty of the night. The great vaulted dome above, set with countless stars of varying lustre, tapered down and apparently lost itself in the distant waters, and on their surface, wrought by the play of wind and wave, appeared crests of silver brightness, sparkling through the semi-gloom. Our ship, with the sails distended and vibrant with motion, plowed steadily on her lonely course in seeming pride and confidence, as though recognizing the grave interests of and responsibility for the many lives entrusted to her keeping.

Friday, May 2d. Awaking about two bells (five o'clock), I was immediately aware of the steady and heavy roll the ship had taken on during the night, and I found myself possessed of an indescribable feeling inclining to nausea, yet with no inclination towards vomiting. I at first thought my condition due to something eaten at dinner the previous day. On attempting to rise, my head seemed to spin around with something of the noise attending the velocity of the wheel of a sewing-machine, my legs seemed to challenge me to risk their support — and, horrors of horrors, it dawned upon me I was seasick! The steward came aft while I was making an effort to roll up my mattress and blanket, and seeing me staggering about, greeted me with an exasperating "Hello, what's the matter?" He had realized my situation at once, and detecting a restrained tickle in his voice, and consoling myself with the thought that his turn would come soon, I answered as bravely as possible, "Nothing." However, there is no such thing as dissembling sea-sickness for any length of time, and I soon acknowledged the "corn," and even tried to produce a smile, which he considerately asked me not to repeat. He then made me a cup of hot tea, of which I drank a little, and throwing an old coat about me, made my way forward to hide my misery in the obscurity of the berth deck. I was for three days perfectly useless and of all persons the most miserable. During the pleasant hours of the afternoon I would drag myself to the foc'sle and lie inactively, braced against the mast and swaying in painful unison with each roll of the ship. At mealtime the steward or cook would seek me out; but food was an unwelcome sight, and, with the exception of soup made by the ship's cook, which in some way supplied a feeling of comfort to the inner man, I tasted nothing. Lemons too, the great alleviator, to which the seasick soul instinctively turns, afforded no relief, and I finally became resigned to let the malady wear itself out in its own way. To those who may not have experienced this exquisite agony, I may say there is no possible danger of not detecting its presence, and when its pleasure has at last been completed no phrase will adequately express the full sense of renewed vigor and animation which possesses one on its departure. On the afternoon of the third day I was sufficiently myself to resume duty and appetite, and, in consideration of the latter, asked the steward to make an extra allowance in his preparations for dinner.

Monday, May 5th. Fine weather still prevailed, and the lapse of each twenty-four hours placed more than two hundred miles to our credit, which was then considered during very well for a man-of-war. All sorts of conjectures and calculations were made as to the time of our arrival at Gibraltar, and numerous bets were made by the men, to be paid when they got ashore on their first liberty. A sailor's life aboard a man-of-war at sea is a busy one, the effect possibly of a time-honored scheme to keep him out of mischief; during his watch in rough weather he is kept constantly on the move, and, when extremely rough, both watches are kept on deck. In pleasant weather, such as prevailed during this trip, the mornings, after quarters, were given over to one or another of the different drills. This morning short-arm practice was ordered; the entire crew filed aft and received their equipment from the armorer, which in this instance was a wooden sword. We then, under an officer in charge, took our position with the company or section to which we belonged on the part of the deck assigned to us. Each one was given a fencing partner, and for an hour the effort to cut, parry, and thrust was made in playful earnestness. In this way the morning passed swiftly, and eight bells proclaiming the welcome hour of dinner was soon heard. This is the meal Jack enjoys most, for whatever he has is hot. Supper is usually made up from the leftover meat from dinner. The smoking lamp remains lighted till two bells (one o'clock), when turn to is sounded and the sweepers piped. I have often wondered since living abroad a man-of-war if housewives really state the fact when they say a room or house does not need sweeping, for, with the scrupulous neatness and cleanliness practiced aboard ship, on sweeping after each meal whole pansful of dirt are taken up, and I suppose it will always remain a puzzle how such quantities regularly accumulate.

At four bells (two o'clock), the apprentices were called aft for school, and the lesson, in charge of one of the senior officers, occupied about an hour, during which, the instructor's attention being attracted now and then to another part of the ship, the opportunity for the working of boyish pranks so characteristic of the schoolroom would be fully improved.

Tuesday, May 6th. The days now were really enjoyable, and if such conditions could be depended on "life on the ocean wave" would indeed be the delightful experience the poet would have us think.

The roughness of the sea, which had for awhile caused some of us to feel a very tender yearning for a life in which no vision of angry waters might obtrude, had given place to the long, gentle, graceful swell, noiseless and rippleless, each in turn seeming only to embrace the ship in evidence of friendliness, and passed under and away to mingle with the myriads that had gone before. Our course lay in the neighborhood of the route most frequented by the European trade, and the occasional "sail ho" of the lookout would bring all hands to the foc'sle to talk and speculate about the stranger which, in some instances, seen only for a short time, across the bright shimmer of water, would disappear below the horizon, or again, as sometimes happened when chancing to travel in a somewhat parallel line, we would keep her in view two or three days, hazarding all possible conjectures as to who or what she is and speaking of her as our friend or companion until, on taking an early look some morning, we find a divergence in course has hid her from sight.

Saturday, May 10th. Yesterday the steward offered up as a sacrifice to appetite the last of our live stock in the shape of two ancient hens. They, however, in keeping with long lives of usefulness, extended their benefactions beyond the one meal, positively refusing to be eaten until the cook's choppers had reduced them to a very palatable hash and served them this morning for breakfast. The cabin larder, however, was not entirely depleted, for there was a supply of eggs packed away in salt sufficient to last until port was reached, and, considering the many forms in which this article may be sent to table, was an invaluable resource in such emergencies.

The ward-room and steerage messes had reached bedrock in this line some days previously, and the stewards of each now spent many sleepless moments in their hammocks studying how to prepare canned goods in the most toothsome manner, and avoid the kick a resentful stomach is sure to bring.

The wardroom steward and cook created quite a breeze in the region of the galley to-day, to the intense delight of the sailors who stood around and in various ways fanned the flames of discord.

It seems that William, as steward, insisted on having the meals prepared as he directed, while Joe, who was a very good cook in all, save one essential, cleanliness, would, though apparently submissive, proceed with all the determined effrontery of which his race is capable, to have his own way. This led to his being reported, and when the case was brought before the captain at the mast, which is the bar of justice aboard ship, the Chinaman was reproved severely, and told that further trouble of that nature would end in his speedy punishment. As Joe turned to go forward the men who had gathered within earshot parted to either side, and he passed through snapping his little eyes in anger. On regaining the galley his pent up feelings overflowed in such phrases as "Gor tam black rascal." "Make a me tire." "I fixa him you bet."

May 11*th*. Sunday, which on shore brings a

period of rest and recreation to thousands of weary toilers, is also aboard a man-of-war a day of restful ease and quiet, and aside from the washing down of the deck by the early watch, and the subsequent cleaning and polishing of bright work for inspection, there is no ship work of any character done.

After breakfast, preparations are made for quarters, soiled work-clothes tucked away out of sight are replaced by clean suits and caps; the cooks are in a fume about the galley for fear they will not be cleaned up by two bells, while the master-at-arms, who is responsible for the appearance of the berth-deck, is on the lookout for some thoughtless fellow who, perhaps, has left his sea-boots or "diddy" box where they should not be.

Quarters over, the men disperse to their different loafing places. The smoking lamp is lighted, and, between a puff and a yarn, their off-watch will be spent by some, while the more industrious will be found seated about deftly quilting a pair of work trousers, weaving a new lanier, or poring over a well-thumbed novel of travel or adventure. The Sunday dinner forward is something of an event, for besides the usual salt junk, the cooks prepare what they call a "duff," which is a pudding made of flour with a few raisins added, and eaten with a sauce made of drawn butter, vinegar, and molasses. To this Jack looks forward with eager pleasure, and, taken a little now and then, is really very good.

I spent a good part of this day with H—— walking fore and aft on the foc'sle, conversing on different topics or running over various French sentences which I endeavored to remember. He was in the same unhappy mind concerning his position and surroundings, hoping and trusting that events might speedily combine to, or some fortunate circumstance effect his release from what he termed a miserable prison.

Monday, May 12*th.* A change in our course was made in the early watch last night, and it is rumored that we are to stop at Fayal before proceeding to Gibraltar. This being true, the run will be shortened several days, and, in less than a week, the present weather continuing, we will reach port. When the hands were turned to this morning, the order was passed to "scrub and wash clothes." The lines were gotten up and wove fore and aft, and in a few moments every part of the deck was alive with men on their knees with pants and sleeves rolled up, feet bare, and clothes spread before them, were repeating the formula of soaping, scrubbing, and rinsing, till the various articles had been cleansed. Each of them strapped his pieces on the line, blue and white clothes separately, and, at the word, they were triced up to flutter about all day, unless rain or the working of ship should render their earlier hauling down necessary. The weather towards evening became quite threatening, heavy banks of black clouds were suspended ominously as though about to burst in angry torrents over the ship; a swelling sea, the waves running high and taking us amidships, pouring a plentiful shower of spray over the deck and causing a considerable roll was the condition, when, at four bells (six o'clock), all hands were called to take in sail.

A storm seemed imminent, and the men followed each other rapidly on deck clad in oilskins and sou'westers. Besides taking in sail, the gallant and royal yards were sent down and secured on deck and all preparations made for a rough night. We ran along for more than an hour, ready for any emergency, weathering an occasional squall of wind and rain, until at last the clouds seemed to lighten and it became apparent we were leaving the storm behind. The sea continued rough during the night, but coming on deck (Tuesday, May. 13th), the weather was again clear and scarcely a trace was visible of the dark visaged clouds of the evening before. The remainder of the trip was completed without incident until about five A. M. on the morning of the 20th, we sighted the island of San Miguel, and, steaming around the coast, anchored at 12.25 in the Bay of Fayal.

Approaching the group known as the "Azores" or Western Islands, the observer becomes impressed with their utter isolation; showing but little stretch of mainland, distinct unto themselves, they rise by an irregular and ragged ascent to heights varying between a thousand and seven thousand feet. The great Atlantic sweeps around and about them, sometimes angrily, as though resentful for their intrusion, and affords an often dangerous highway for transportation from one to another.

As our vessel rounds the southernmost point of the Island of Fayal, upon which is placed a signal station, there lies before us a scene of undoubted beauty; the capital city, Horta, situated near the entrance to the crescent-shaped harbor, stretches itself along the shore and has encroached to some extent on the mountain side, while the cultivated gardens and thick growth of trees and shrubbery at a higher elevation form a background of luxuriant richness for the quaint little tile-roofed, white painted dwellings brightly reflecting the summer sun. Quite a number of smaller crafts carrying passengers or loaded with merchandise were being propelled rapidly from place to place and furnished an element of traffic and industry to an otherwise quiet scene. A thick stone wall has been built around the beach as a protection against the ravages of the seas, and, unlike the almost useless breakwater which stands but partially completed at the entrance to the harbor, is a finished work, solid and enduring.

We anchored about a mile from the jetty and shortly after received a visit from the American consul, Mr. Dabney, in whose family the representation of the United States in these islands has rested almost successively for nearly seventy years.

After lunch the captain told the steward he might go ashore and see what was to be had in the way of fresh provisions, adding that I might go along if I wished; we hailed one of the shore boats, several of which were paddling about near the ship in anticipation of a fare, and in a few moments were landed at the wharf in the midst of a scene full of life and color, boats being loaded and unloaded, men, women, and children with baskets or boxes filled with some kind of produce moving here and there and still many others pursuing the more agreeable occupation of doing nothing.

Very little interest was manifested in ourselves except by a few ragged boys who considered there might be a penny or so to pick up, and leaving the wharf with one of the boatmen as guide we started to take a near view of the city. Fayal with its sister islands has belonged to Portugal since early in the 15th century, and its inhabitants are entirely of that nationality. The people are generally poor and of peaceful, quiet habits; the arrival of a strange vessel in the bay, the approach of which is heralded by the signal station, forms the most exciting incident and has a corresponding effect on the people as that of a circus parading the streets of an American town. We followed our guide along the principal street, which takes the direction of the bay to the money-changers, where in exchange for a bright gold piece we received a sack full of curious looking brass and copper coins of the relative value of which we were extremely doubtful, and then visited several dingy looking shops all stocked with a miscellaneous assortment of dry goods, fruit, fish, tobacco, and vegetables; in each of these the keeper sat idly by as if more from habit than any idea he might have that his services would be needed. We were confronted with several phases of native life during our brief walk; there are no pavements, and in the road, which is of a hard, smooth substance and quite free from dust, one steps aside to allow passage for a team of frisky donkeys, or a female returning from the well, with a water jar on her head, moving steadily on with graceful evenness of a modern cakewalker; again are seen women enveloped with cloaks of ample fold and reaching to their feet, the head encased in hoods * several times larger than our grandmothers' sun-bonnets.

The average visitor sees very little of the business life of Fayal and he is very apt to wonder how the people support themselves; to be sure they are kept very busy going to church, but, notwithstanding this, much time is also spent back in the hills where there are many rich groves of oranges and gardens under perfect cultivation. Our stay ashore at this time was shorter than we could have wished, but duty was imperative and promising ourselves a possible visit next day, returned to the wharf, made a few purchases and went aboard the ship.

I was awakened about four o'clock next morning by an unusual noise and the hum of strange voices coming from the side of the ship, and looking out the pantry port I beheld a large coal lighter alongside and knew that the disagreeable process of coaling ship was about to begin. Immediately closing the deadlights, ports, and transoms to exclude as much dust as possible from the cabin, I went forward to take an early view of the surroundings. Seldom has nature

---

* This costume casually seen by the traveler resembles that worn by the sisters of some religious order, but if one be sufficiently near to obtain a view of the face the idea is at once *dispelled*, for if there are two in company he sees pleasant smiling faces lighted with the sparkle of conversation and in which evidences are not lacking of a very lively interest in their immediate surroundings.

furnished a more grandly beautiful scene than that which lay before me on this morning; the soft gray of the early twilight falling gently as a gauzy veil over mountain and gorge, and showing houses and wharf and steepled churches in a mellow dimness; revealing the outline of the huge form of Mount Pico across the bay, but partially seen in the hazy distance, its cone lost in mist and standing impressively as a watchful guardian over the peaceful harbor. Soon and almost suddenly, the encompassing pall began to lift, and then a flood of glorious sunshine, bathing the surrounding regions of hills and dales and sending its rays far out along the distant waters, ushered in another day.

With the coming of the early market boat from Pico the inhabitants of the city seemed to resume their daily rounds of work and play, gossip and lounging; the boats were unloaded at the wharf in the midst of a crowd of barefoot children, men without coats, whose trousers were patched or in need of patches; women pattering about in wooden clogs, the noise of which was only equaled by their lively chatter, each taking a basket filled with vegetables or fish or luscious fruit upon their heads and hastening to the market place. The ship's "dingey" was called away to take the stewards ashore to market at five o'clock, who were happy in escaping for awhile the many discomforts of coaling; a dozen or more Portuguese laborers had the work in charge under the direction of a boss or overseer, and worked persistently and untiringly, singing and talking all the while. By twelve o'clock the coal bunkers had been filled and every trace of the dirty process removed; decks holystoned, paint scrubbed, and bright work shining. After lunch the captain said we might spend the afternoon ashore,* he having accepted an invitation to dine with the consul that evening. The permission being general as far as the cabin folks were concerned, we told Louis to hurry and get ready, and a little later we were being pulled rapidly ashore. The fort being near the wharf, we looked in upon the handful of seedy soldiers lounging about clad in a pretense of uniform, or engaged in some kind of a game; rare specimens of the war implements of a remote age were mounted here and there in neighborly intimacy with several mounds of rusty cannon balls, while the general lack of even a semblance of discipline on the part of the meagre garrison forced the conclusion that for these people "grim visaged war" existed only in fancy, and that the fort is only retained as a concession to the war spirit of the age. In our wanderings we passed several old stone buildings, their sides mossgrown and streaked with damp, doors and window frames shrunken from their settings, and generally most wofully dilapidated. We learned through various inquiries that they were more than four hundred years old, and had originally been used as monasteries, which were abolished during the regency of Dom Pedro I of Portugal; in later years they were used as garrisons. We took a hasty view of one of the

---

* The regulations governing "liberty" or going ashore do not apply to the captain's people, and, so long as their conduct is first-class, they are privileged to go whenever the captain does not need them.

churches: the interior dimly lighted, the altar and chancel decorated with faded hangings and religious vestments, a flooring of plain broad boards and damp dingy walls, and the two confessionals on either side of the entrance, made up a whole severely suggestive of an oppressed state of moral and mental growth; there are, however, several church buildings on the islands of much greater architectural importance in which finely-executed carvings, priestly vestments of some costliness, and richly inlaid mosiacs, representing various church ordinances, combine to make an interior of great beauty and attractiveness.

Being in a neighborhood where traces are not wanting showing the dire result of the fateful phenomena of volcanoes, we were not content to leave the opportunity unimproved by at least a somewhat closer view. The distance to the base of the mountains was five miles or more, and although the way was very rough the extraordinary beauty and diversity of the scenery was such as to enchain our fancy and lead us willingly on insensible to fatigue. The lateness of the hour did not admit of an extended climbing of the ascent, but a height was gained from which immense fissures made by the lava current were plainly visible, while forming their beds were masses of hardened cinders or solid rock; the earth about was covered with a hard granulated substance exceedingly light and of brownish color, presumably a form of matter sent out during an eruption, and which easily loosened or started from a position rendered a foothold very insecure, while about on all sides were layers of rocks and here and there a scrubby patch of moss or stunted bush.* From our elevation we looked through a vista composed of rugged trees, all kinds of variegated plants, little houses of one or two rooms dotted here and there, and at the base a stream issuing out of the mountains, on the banks of which were the washerwomen pursuing their vocation and children merrily paddling in the water; to complete this perfect scene we looked beyond the bridge which spans the stream, the great Atlantic rolls peacefully along, and then our view is broken by the majestic snow-capped form of Pico. Twilight was fast approaching as we descended the mountain, and gaining the road, fell in with a straggling procession of natives returning to the city from their day's work.

Our little excursion, the effects of which we were beginning to feel, came to an end at the wharf, and in due time we were again aboard ship, where we sought without great delay a most welcome rest. We left this beautiful place at midday on the 22d, carrying with us pleasant memories of our brief visit, with the unceasing noise of the water breaking against the harbor walls sounding in our ears and the form of Pico lingering in the view as we steamed eastward towards Gibraltar.

---

* We were informed that strangers often visited the crater, making the trip on donkeys, which are reputed safe and steady climbers. The greater part of the day is necessary for its completion.

ROCK OF GIBRALTER.

CHAPTER V.

GIBRALTAR.

THE passage from Fayal to Gibraltar was made in five days, during which pleasant weather prevailed, and each day bringing us nearer the Mediterranean, the great highway of European travel; our leisure moments were almost constantly employed watching the many vessels sighted from time to time. Early on the morning of the 26th, Cape St. Vincent, the extreme southwest point of Portugal was made, and about 5 A. M., on the 27th, the now familiar cry of "land ahead" again greeted our ears, and we had come in view of the northwest coast of Africa. A few hours later, the rock of Gibraltar, the pillar of Hercules to the ancients, and an enduring monument to the heroes of the naval battle of 1805, stands before us — heavy, solemn, formidable. Our anchorage in Gibraltar bay is reached about noon and the harbor is found well filled with the vessels of different nations; England is represented by an enormous ram and two other war ships, while the flags of France, Germany, and Japan are floating from the gaffs of gunboats in different parts of the bay. The merchant marine is also strongly in evidence; all of which with the many smaller craft, ferry boats, lighters, steam launches, sail boats, and smaller ships; boats flitting here and there, in every direction, make up a scene of lively and exciting interest to the stranger.

About two o'clock the captain received a visit from Mr. Sprague, the American consul, and following close upon each other the ranking officer of the fort and the commanders of the other war vessels paid their respects to the latest arrival. The afternoon was passed in preparations on the part of the crew for the work which was to begin on the morrow. A beautiful evening, with a balmy breeze blowing over the bay succeeded a pleasant day and was spent chiefly on the forecastle singing, talking, and watching the many lights on shore and about the harbor, until two bells (nine o'clock), when the clear mellow bugle notes from the different war ships sounding "taps," rang out clear and sweet across the water, and died away in lingering echoes among the hills around.

The men were set to work early next morning tarring down the rigging, after which painting ship was in order; the cabin carpets, which had been taken up on leaving Norfolk, were relaid, and in every way the vessel was made to present a bright and cheery appearance. The men turned to with a hearty good will and dispatched the work in about half the usual time. "Liberty" was in the air, for more than a month had passed since Jack was ashore, and in anticipation he already sipped the fragrant juice of Andalusia or quaffed the "bloomin' mug of 'alf and 'alf." The paymaster issued an allowance of money in the afternoon, and the word was passed that the starboard watch would go ashore on thirty-six hours' liberty, beginning next morning at nine o'clock.

My friend H———, who was in that watch, before going ashore placed the books he had spoken of some time since in my care, saying if anything happened to him they would serve to remind me of an absent friend. And now, reader, while the crew are ashore paying tribute at the shrine of Bacchus, let you and me take a look at this famous place. You doubtless know that Gibraltar is a fortified rock on the extreme southern coast of Spain and the boasted possession of Great Britain. It is, at its highest point, about 1,400 feet above sea level. The north side presents an unbroken surface of steep, barren rock while the east and south sides are of ragged and uneven appearance extremely difficult of approach; on the western side, which is of a gradual slope, is built the town of Gibraltar, overlooking the bay of the same name. The rock is joined to the main land by a low sandy isthmus separating the sea from Gibraltar bay. From two rows of sentry boxes on either edge of a narrow strip of the isthmus called "neutral ground," England and Spain watch each other with a jealous eye, for Spain has ever been Britain's unwilling neighbor. The bay of Gibraltar, which is formed by the rock on the east and the main land of Spain on the west as it reaches out to the point St. Garcia at the extreme south, is about four miles wide and five long; directly opposite, on the western arm of the bay, is the Spanish town of Algeceiras.

The Strait of Gibraltar, the passageway between

the Atlantic and the Mediterranean, is thirty-six miles long and has a maximum width of thirteen miles, while nine miles is the distance between the two coasts at its narrowest point opposite Tarifa. The western slope of the rock, nearest the strait, is reserved exclusively for the purposes of the garrison, and here are located the barracks and the smaller parade grounds. To the north a colony of English resident officials are quartered in a style becoming their station as representatives of a powerful government, while the city proper has been given the advantage of a greater incline of surface towards the northern end of the rock, and is thereby enabled to have a principal highway called "Main" street, less than three-quarters of a mile long, while there are three or four extremely short ones cutting it at right angles. At the base of the precipitous bluff, which forms the northern front, there stretches out to the "neutral ground" a narrow neck of land which forms the principal parade ground of the English garrison.

The inhabitants of the rock are Spanish, English, Jews, and Moors. The last-named, being in easy distance of their home across the strait, make frequent trips back and forth, and as poulterers furnish the greater part of such supplies consumed in the town. It is said that Spanish Gibraltar is ever watchful of the Moor, as instances are not wanting of his having wreaked summary vengeance on account of some real or fancied wrong. The female population hold them in especial fear, and an intimation of their approach is sufficient cause for the immediate locking and barring of doors.

Disturbances, however, are very rare, considering the different nationalities often thrown together in this small place, especially when, as often happens, the crews of different vessels are ashore at the same time; for though sailors are ordinarily peaceable, when on liberty they cast off all restraint, and are determined to enjoy to the uttermost and at any cost their brief independence. In convivial moods, it has been the case that a question of relative merit, an unthinking boast, or a slighting reference to a rival, have furnished ample pretext for a lively and at times sanguinary encounter.

There is something peculiarly attractive about Gibraltar, and although outside of the fort one may easily traverse every inch of ground in less than half a day, there may be spent several days before its many quaint and altogether unique features will be exhausted. The greatest engineering as well as architectural skill has been brought to bear in adapting the unusual surface to the needs of buildings, resident and otherwise, in which the prerequisite of comfort has not been ignored, and the rigid necessity for economy of space has been so artfully dealt with as to develop upon examination many surprises. There are three hotels whose accommodations are in no sense first class, although the proprietors and retainers are heartily in earnest in their efforts to please, and at the "King's Arms," where I took lodging for one night, having been late for the last boat going off to the ship, I had the pleasure of a very comfortable bed, whose downy texture and generous size were delightfully soothing after a month's hard jolting and rolling on shipboard.

The spiritual welfare of the inhabitants should be well cared for, inasmuch as there are several Catholic and Protestant churches, besides three or four Jewish synagogues. The government hospital, located on one of the little cross streets which takes the name of Hospital Ramp, is a commodious structure, scrupulously clean and neat, and in which the highest degree of efficiency is maintained in every department. Among other public buildings are storehouses, schools, a lunatic asylum, and a theatre, in which Spanish opera by a celebrated troupe from Madrid was presented during our stay. My first visit ashore was of rather an unpleasant nature, for I was in search of a dentist. I found him in the person of an old gray-haired and bearded man, certainly not less than seventy years of age and apparently very feeble, so much so that I doubted his ability to extract the offending member, a very stout molar. I could not make him understand my fears, for he was Spanish and I was something else, so I concluded to have him make the trial at all hazards, for anything was better than the exquisite bit of torture I was then enduring. He selected his instrument and in the coolest possible manner proceeded to carve himself a holding place for the forceps, with which, taking a firm grip, he forthwith began to pull with such determined energy that it dawned upon me he meant to have either my head or the tooth, and in a few seconds the tooth gracefully yielded, to my great relief.

Of all the points of interest about the rock, the fortress naturally attracts the greatest attention from visitors, and one may easily spend all of two days in looking over its many wonderful features. The soldier who does escort duty is very attentive, and if he thinks you "true blue," and may be depended on for a generous tip the ingenious mechanism of this world-famed place are uncovered to the view.

From the harbor one sees strange looking holes of irregular shape and at different elevations on the rock, giving no evidence of design, but appearing more as the result of some natural condition; on visiting the fort they are seen to be the port-holes through which the latest improved and most powerful cannon may be trained at any moment. The great galleries tunneled through the solid rock are of sufficient size for the easy handling of the large guns, while about the heaviest batteries have been built vaults and trenches as additional security against exploding shells. Besides the evidences of engineering skill which are indeed remarkable, there are a number of natural caverns, in one of which, called St. Michael's, stalactites have formed and hang in various lengths and fantastic shapes from every part of the roof.

On the summit of the highest peak is placed the signal station, commanding a view of many miles in all directions, and this station is also a medium of telegraph to all important points on the rock, while along the crest and pointed threateningly over the western slope are several of the largest batteries.

This stronghold has been an element of contention between nations ever since the advantage of its position was discovered by the Saracens early in the eighth century. A merry warfare was waged during many years between Moor and Christian, with Gibraltar as the stake, when, in the fourteenth century, Spain took a hand, a new deal was made, and the game which had now become most exciting was finally brought to a finish by Great Britain "sitting out" her opponents, France and Spain, in the memorable siege of four years, ending in 1783. There are no business enterprises or industries carried on at the rock, the population ekeing out a precarious living through the many ships which enter the harbor for coal or shelter, a lively contraband traffic with Spain, and by catering to the social needs of the English soldiery. The neighborhood affords an abundance of delicious fruit and vegetables of several kinds, while the beef which is brought across the strait from Tangier is extremely poor. The strictest scrutiny is maintained over the movements of strangers, who are required to have a pass, while the most stringent regulations are enforced seeking to prevent the too rapid increase of the resident population.

The visitor, having exhausted the attractions of the rock, may engage one of the public carriages (several of which are always found promenading Main street), and for a few shillings he may be whirled along the bleached and hardened roadway, past "neutral ground," where for a moment the "Jehu" pulls up in front of the Spanish sentry to give his passenger a "clean bill," and then pushing ahead, belaboring his poor though willing steed at every step, he in a short while reaches Spanish Town. The inhabitants of this little place are keenly alive to the main chance; the clatter and rattle of the rickety vehicle, accompanied by the noise of unshod hoof, have heralded a new arrival, and the proprietors of wineshops from their doorway smile a most seductive welcome, while the couriers for other attractions with wild gesture and noisy speech endeavor to convince the driver of the superiority of their several claims. It is needless to say that this important person "stands in" with all hands and is sure of his fee in any case.

The visitor seldom lingers long in Spanish Town; the streets are filthy and the entire tone of the place is exceedingly low. It is something of a military town and contains low, rambling, yellow-painted barracks, about which a squad of soldiers sit or lounge in the shade of the court and engage in contests of smoke puffed from their pipes or cigarettes. The drive may be continued to the town of San Roque, a few miles further north, or by following the road which skirts the bay one reaches the charming little town of Algeceiras.

A muster of the starboard watch when "liberty" was up, disclosed five unwarranted absences. Among the number was friend H——; none of the boys remembered to have seen him during their stay ashore, and his non-appearance aboard ship was all the more singular as he was considered a model character and not known to indulge in any of the vices to which sailors usually lend themselves when ashore. Among a few particular friends, the deepest concern was felt, as they thought his love for adventure might have led him to make a journey inland on the Spanish side and that he might have been foully dealt with. The usual notice was sent to the authorities ashore, with descriptions, and offering ten dollars reward, which resulted in the return of three of the delinquents.

Friend H—— and a Portuguese sailor named Fernandez were the missing, and the idea occurred to me that possibly the former's words in giving into my keeping the books, "they will serve to remind you of an absent friend," were significant, and that, perhaps, it was his pleasure to be missing; in any case "he never came back," and among a few of us who knew him intimately, the loss was keenly felt.

The port watch was given their turn ashore, and having been duly posted by their friends of the other watch, had the advantage of not being entirely strange, and started in with buoyant spirits for their thirty-six hours spree. The Captain, who was the recipient of much social attention, gave the steward orders for a series of luncheons and dinners, which kept us busy several days. These functions having been discharged satisfactorily, we were accorded abundant privilege in the matter of going ashore, and in this respect we fared particularly well throughout the cruise.

A person finding himself in a foreign city, especially where a strange language is spoken, is very often placed at serious disadvantage. The money being also strange, aside from the risk of being exorbitantly charged, he very often, through ignorance of values, pays more than is really charged.

There are then, generally, men who, self-appointed perhaps, act as guides and protectors, and experience justifies the belief that is far better for the pocket to be the victim of one person, who, if you make him fair promises, will protect you against all others, than to wander aimlessly, here and there, a shining mark for the greed of the ever watchful and unscrupulous.

Upon reaching the Ragged Staff landing in company with C——, a few days after our arrival in port, we were accosted familiarly with the words "How do you do, gentlemen; can I do anything for you?" The speaker was a young Spaniard, apparently about twenty-one, of pleasing address and using the English tongue easily and well. Without allowing us time to refuse or accept his services, he proceeded to tell us any number of facts about the Rock, and finally introduced himself as Domingo, adding that his time was his own and intimating that any part of it was ours to command. He remained with us throughout the evening, and then, as also during the succeeding days, proved himself invaluable as guide and friend.

When separating at the landing, he told us of the *Corridas de toras*, which was to take place the Sunday following across the bay at Algeceiras, and which would also mark the opening of the annual fair. We had often heard of the Spanish bull-fight, and to have one within easy reach and not witness it, was scarcely to be thought of.

We met our new friend Domingo per agreement at the Ragged Staff, about one o'clock Sunday, the first of June. The weather was extremely hot, and in fact a day on which one's clothes seem inspired with a clinging fondness, and on which the remembrance of shady nooks and sylvan glades come with crushing and unwelcome vividness. The streets seemed deserted as we made our way towards the ferry, for those who had not gone to the fair were quietly enjoying their siesta within latticed halls or shaded courts. Our patience was severely taxed by the little side-wheeler which ferried us over, for an hour and a half was used in making the six miles, and scarcely waiting for her to make fast to the wharf, the crowd scrambled ashore and hastened away to the fair grounds.

Our haste did not prevent a feeling of genuine admiration for this pretty little city, for in direct contrast to its neighbor, Spanish Town, the people here seemed to divide their homage between pleasure and cleanliness. The principal street was shaded by a row of trees on either side, and in their rear was a succession of charming little white and green painted cottages. Spanish architecture delights in balconies, and these in various forms were noticed, and the imagination might easily supply the other romantic essentials of love, moonlight, a serenade, and pretty girls. Further along, a turn in the road has brought us in view of the fair grounds, and the eye is filled with an immense stretch of sloping turf so generously shaded as to almost cheat one with the belief that some dark and evenly colored material had been spread in tender protection of nature's virgin green. A smooth stone pavement, twenty or thirty feet wide, extended through the center towards the amphitheatre, while on either side was a row of trees whose foliage joined overhead and formed a royal arch, beneath which an excited crowd of pleasure seekers hurried towards the scene of the performance.

In the vicinity of the amphitheatre, of which we

soon gained a view, were scattered many small booths and tents, varying in size from that occupied by the patent lemonade mixer, to the one in which the *corp de' ballet* was causing roguish smiles to furrough the bald heads of several score of country jays.

The "sure thing" and "straight tip" manipulators reaped a golden harvest, and with the pure brass of fearlessness invited the multitude to become wealthy at their expense. Around the enclosure, sweltering, unprotected from the sun's rays, and moving in wedge-like motion through the various entrances, were dusty, impatient, and noisy crowds, male and female of all ages and conditions. Through the pulling of some unseen wire by our companion, Domingo, we escaped a tedious wait, and were admitted after the purchasing of tickets through a reserved entrance. This "pull" was, however, not sufficiently vigorous to seat us in the grand stand, and we had to content ourselves with seeing the show from the "bleachers." The structure was entirely of wood, plainly and almost roughly built, and with seating room for eight thousand. The seats, of ordinary deal boards, rose tier upon tier to the outer rim. A stout barrier encircled the ring, serving as a partition between spectators and performers, and on the ring side of this were built, equally distant one from the other, a number of wooden screens or slides, the use of which became apparent later on.

Already a vast audience was becoming restless, and the few remaining seats were being rapidly taken. In the Governor's box were a dozen or more ladies and gentlemen, the latter in military costume, while the grand stand, the lower portion of which served for the band, was completely filled with a choice company of the votaries of the national pastime, representing the nobility and fashion of provincial society.

Forgetting time and surroundings, one might easily imagine the scene one of our fashionable theatres, for with like display of costly jewels and elegant raiment do these ardent Spaniards attend this performance; aside from these species of adornment, the native charm of manner inherent with Spanish women, the dark flashing eye, wealth of raven hair, and the innumerable elements of grace and attractiveness, which are as natural with them as the delicate and often unconscious motion of their fan, combined to make a scene of bewildering interest and beauty. Packed in among the thousands of persons seated on the unsheltered boards, many of whom placed handkerchiefs in their hats or around their necks for protection from the sun, we awaited the performance, while in and out, from bench to bench, and over the shoulders of the spectators, refreshment venders made their way crying their wares with lusty tones.

CHAPTER VI.

THE BULL FIGHT.

THE musicians mounting to their places was the signal for a demonstration of hand clapping, and a moment later men with water cans appeared and thoroughly sprinkled the arena. The band struck up a lively air, and at the same time the performance was heralded by a tiny baby jockey riding skillfully and at a rapid gait around the ring. He completed the circuit several times and finally pulled up in approved style and saluted before the Governor's box.

Upon the exit of the little actor the trumpets sound, the gates swing open, and two horsemen with velvet capes and plumed hats gallop forward and uncover before his Excellency with knightly courtesy, and ask permission for the performance to take place, which with the key to the bull pen is immediately given.

This is followed by prolonged applause, and the two knights having returned to the entrance, a shrill blast is blown from the horns, the drums beat, and while every eye is strained to catch a first view, the gates open and the procession enters. Three matadores, one of whom is Mazantini, a man celebrated throughout Spain for his prowess in this line, follow in the wake of the two knights who have taken the lead; they are dressed in suits of black velvet trimmed with gilt embroidery. Pumps and white stockings adorn their feet and legs, while a bunch of colored ribbons is noticed at the knee. The banderilleros, eight in number, follow clad in velvets of different colors and each carrying what appeared to be a red cloak suspended from the arm.

Now come the picadors, whose mounts were the poorest apologies obtainable in a country where even a fairly good horse is rare. Their trappings, however, were gay and the display was not wholly lost upon them, for they seemed to lift their feet a little higher under the spell of martial music.

Three very large mules, affording a notable contrast to their puny cousins and decked with flowers and jingling bells, brought up the rear, and were used to drag the dead and disabled from the ring. Twice the tour was made, after which the music ceased, the mules were driven back to their quarters, and a flourishing of trumpets announced the beginning of the fray.

The picadors, with lance in readiness, took positions opposite the side from whence the bull would come, and now there seemed to be a moment of absolute quiet; the vast throng in a fever of expectancy scarcely breathed. The signal being given and the gates opened, the bull, furious by confinement and enraged with hunger, nostrils distended and eyes flaming, bounded into the center of the ring. The crowd is now wild with delight, for they see he possesses the real untamed metal, and great sport may be expected.

The animal stood for a brief moment, shifting his eyes restlessly along the line of horsemen, as though deciding upon a point of attack; suddenly, and with a half-suppressed bellow, he rushed and plunged upon the nearest picador, who braced himself and, adjusting his lance, endeavored to repel the onslaught. The savage brute, now fully aroused, pressed the attack, and catching the horse upon his horns, threw man and beast to the ground.

The picador was unable to extricate himself, having fallen beneath, and would have been gored to death but for the intervention of the banderilleros, who, hurrying to the rescue, were successful in enticing the furious beast from further assault by means of their flaunting cloaks. During the few seconds, when the unhorsed picador seemed in the most *extreme* peril, the audience gazed in fearful expectancy, being incapable of either motion or utterance, until relief from imminent danger brought relaxation, then the joyful outburst from many throats and the waving of hats and fans voiced a most general and hearty satisfaction. The bull turned upon his tormentors of the red cloaks, dashed after one then another, who scampered away flirting their cloaks before him, when, directing his attention to a particular one, he started in for a determined chase. It was a race for life and overpowering in excitement. The man realized his desperate position and, throwing away his cloak, bent every energy in the effort to outstrip his pursuer. The animal gained every second, and with another five feet of distance his horns would have found a sheath of flesh; but the slide, without a second to spare, was reached, and behind it the man threw himself, exhausted, but safe, while his pursuer, scraping the slide as he rushed madly by, came to a stand near the middle of the ring, panting and pawing the earth. The interest awakened by this test of speed, with life and a horrible death as the stake, was painful in its intensity.

The poor horse which was made the object of the first attack was finally gotten on his feet with his entrails protruding from great holes in his abdomen, and in this condition was mounted and made to stand ready against another attack. Ah! what savage cruelty, what inhumanity is this that can make a pastime of such frightful scenes, that can wreathe the lip in smiles and clothe speech in unseemly jest, while poor dumb animals are blindfolded and spurred remorselessly to their death.

The bull is not allowed time to recover from his recent exertion; the sport is continued by the picadors urging their horses towards him and when sufficiently near thrusting their lances deep into his body, when, maddened with pain and the scent of blood, he dashes at them again probing the horses mercilessly, but rarely injuring the men. A notably shocking incident occurred, when a poor animal was forced to his feet with the blood pouring from his wounds as from a pump; the picador mounted notwithstanding, and while digging his spurs into his flanks he sunk to the ground and died in a few moments.

After awhile the picadors leave the ring and the horses are driven or led out, leaving their dead companions where they had fallen. The banderilleros now have the arena; they are armed with an instrument made of a thin round piece of wood having a sharp point of steel.

They are about three feet long and are used one in each hand. The fact that these banderilla are so short requires that they be used at very close range, and the men handling them are of necessity extremely agile and dextrous. They take a position immediately in front of the bull, and as he approaches with lowered head their arms are extended towards him, and when sufficiently near both hands descend together, and these metal-tipped arrows are imbedded with unerring stroke back of the neck and on either side of the spine. With a bellow of pain the animal lifts his head and rushes madly forward while his tormentor has nimbly stepped aside. Soon with numerous arrows stuck into his body and the blood trickling from his wounds, the poor beast seemed almost exhausted, and, standing as if dazed and uncertain which way to turn, gave vent to his distress in a series of mournful bellowing. And now comes that which, in the estimation of the lovers of this sport, is considered the most interesting exhibition of human skill. The matadore, Mazantini,* the hero of the hour, the idol of the populace, and the proud possessor of decorations and honors innumerable, won before crowned heads and high officials in the arenas of Madrid and Seville, enters the ring. His appearance elicits cheer upon

---

* Our party was presented to Mazantini just before taking the ferry to Gibraltar, at which time he handed us each a photo from one of which the accompanying cut is made.

cheer, which is hushed as he advances towards the Governor's box and expresses himself as ready to dispatch the bull in the most approved manner. He is clad in a knee pants suit of black velvet. A generous display of snowy shirt with ruffled front and cuffs relieve the otherwise sombre tone of his dress. In his left hand he holds a piece of scarlet cloth and in his right a small sharp blade of brightest steel.

The poor beast, now weakened by loss of blood and spiritless through suffering, is with difficulty urged to a show of animation.

The matadore, watching closely every movement, advanced towards him waving the blade concealed beneath the cloth with serpent-like motion. With an angry snort the bull plunged desperately towards him, and he, taking one step to the rear, dropped his weapon, and looking the furious animal squarely in the eyes threw up both hands as in benediction. The bull stopped suddenly in his tracks within a few feet of the matadore, and as if doing the resistless bidding of some powerful agent, reared himself slowly on his hindmost feet, and in this extraordinary position remained several seconds, while the throng at length grasping the unusual spectacle broke forth in a delirium of shouting and applause.*

When he had resumed his position upon all fours, the matadore again advanced towards him with blade concealed as before, whereupon the animal sunk forward upon his forelegs in a state of exhaustion with

---

* This spectacle was looked upon as almost marvelous and recognized as an extreme instance of the fascination held by a superior intelligence over the brute creation.

the many wounds bleeding profusely, and from these on all sides protruding the sharp instruments of torture. The end was now near; the stubborn spirit was about to succumb to the inevitable and add another unavailing protest against this more than barbarous pastime.

With a great show of bravado, the master from in front of the resistless animal took exact and steady aim, and with wonderful strength of wrist and unerring stroke plunged the blade its whole length into the body of the beast. The work, according to popular esteem, was most skillfully done, as the animal rolled over instantly at the feet of its slayer.

The band then struck up, the ladies waved their fans and kerchiefs in graceful appreciation of the matadore's art, while the male portion of the audience were frantic with delight, yelling and embracing one another and wildly tossing their hats into the arena.

The mule team was then driven in and the dead and wounded animals hooked on and dragged, amid the whoopings of the drivers, from the ring. This performance which I have attempted to describe was repeated with variations of details six times; nearly a score of horses were killed and wounded.

Charming women, who would ordinarily step out of their way in their eagerness to avoid inflicting pain, sat there unmoved, except to applaud, and witnessed a butchery worse than savages employ. Men accounted noble by the world's interpreting, gazed with fevered interest as the play proceeded, taking a fiendish pleasure in this carnival of blood. For myself, it was an experience upon which the mind will never need to be refreshed, as the slightest reference brings before it vividly every detail which combined to make a panorama of horror and inhumanity.

It was about seven o'clock when we left the amphitheatre: the last lingering rays of the setting sun fell in softened tones bespeaking approaching twilight. A welcome sea breeze had freed nature from the effects of the recent torrid heat.

We made our way through the fair grounds among a merry crowd of pleasure-makers, grand dames, and courtly men, and those of the humbler walks of life jostled each other good naturedly while reviewing the exciting incident of the recent exhibition.

The scene was rich with life and color, the booths gaily decorated, lanterns designed in fancy colors swinging from the trees; while over all the charm of music floated, touching with its powerful magic the closing moments of this fete day of southern Spain.

CHAPTER VII.

ATTRACTIONS AT PALERMO AND MESSINA.

OUR stay at Gibraltar was now drawing to a close, for on the morrow we would resume our sail towards the Orient.

Nothing had been heard of H——, and the Portuguese sailor, Fernandez, had gotten himself in serious trouble and would have to answer to the Spanish authorities to the charge of deadly assault. It was shown that he had engaged in a drunken altercation with a Spanish soldier, in which the latter had been dangerously stabbed. The authorities imprisoned the offender, and every effort to secure his release by our Captain and the American Consul proved unavailing, so that we were reluctantly compelled to leave him behind.

The injuries of the soldier, however, did not result fatally, and after several weeks confinement Fernandez was sent back to America by the Consul, where he was duly punished for his offense through regular departmental procedure.

Our last day in port was employed in taking on stores and the usual preparations for sea, which, in this instance, were somewhat modified, seeing that our next harbor was Palermo, only four or five days' distant. The afternoon was spent by the Captain and officers in making their "P. P. C.'s," for in the interchange of social and official courtesy during these twelve days many friendships had been formed, which the exigencies of naval service alone prevented attaining a more complete growth. Shortly before sundown, there steamed into the harbor the *Arabia*, one of Her British Majesty's troop-ships, homeward bound, with enlisted people, whose term of service in the East Indies had expired. To those of us who had never seen such an enormous vessel, the sight was very interesting. An idea of the capacity of these convoys may be had from the fact that the *Arabia* carried 300 horses, 1,500 soldiers, and 500 women and children, making a total, with ship officers and sailors, of nearly 2,500 souls.

She was of three decks, painted entirely white, and with double funnels fore and aft amidships, from which the smoke poured in dense volumes as she steamed to an anchorage. Cary and I went ashore after dinner to bid adieu to friends, several of whom had been at great pains to make our stay enjoyable. It was with sincere regret we looked forward to leaving a place in which we had for the first time enjoyed full and complete freedom, had men grasp us squarely by the hand as men, and our intellectual and moral statures measured by our attainments rather than by the color of our skin. The notion impressed itself on my mind that persons living under this old world civilization are more truly the arbiters of their destiny, inasmuch as they have not that accursed prejudice to contend against which says how far one shall or shall not come.

At 10 A. M. on the morning of the 13th, "all hands" were piped "up anchor," and by noon we had left the Rock behind and were steaming eastward over the blue waters of the Mediterranean. For two days we ran along in view of the African coast, during which we traced its barren and sandy outline and I thought of the myriads of Afric's sons who had trod this soil, of the mighty rulers who in ages past built great cities, cultivated the arts of peace and war, and finally went their way to mingle their dust with those who had gone before. It has been aptly said: "We build with what we call eternal rock; a distant age asks where the fabric stood, and in the dust sifted and searched in vain the undiscoverable secret sleeps."

The many duties incident to the sea and to the extended mechanism of a man-of-war were taken up as though no intermission filled with the manifold attractions and allurements of life ashore had occurred. The prospect of a few days of comparative rest was more than welcome, and the interchange of recent experiences between individuals or among groups of interested listeners, filled in our leisure moments while speeding over an almost rippleless sea.

The usual drills of small arms or broad swords were gone through each morning, with the exception that on the 17th we went to target practice, and for two hours the different gun crews were drilled in this principle of naval warfare.

The weather was favorable for the practice, bright and sunshiny, with a smooth sea whose sparkling expanse of phosphorescent blue was only broken here and there by a rising swell flecked into foam by wind and current. The target, which was in the form of a cube made of canvas and rigged upon a frame work of wood, was dropped astern, and the vessel steamed away to a distance of about a thousand yards from whence operations began. The effect of the different shots was watched by all hands with considerable interest; a loud report, an instant's flash, and a puff of smoke, and the deadly missile is sent on its way; for a few seconds we follow its course through the air and see it drop into the water, near the target—perhaps. After several shots had been fired with varying result, the target was picked up (undamaged) and the ship was brought up again to her course.

We arrived at Palermo at 4.30 on the afternoon of the 18th. Within an ample breakwater, we found anchored many vessels, principally yachts and merchantmen, while the *Ossipee* had the distinction of being the only war vessel in port. The view from the harbor is most picturesque. The city, which is rather compactly built, is situated at the southwest end of the large bay in an extensive tract, which, from the luxuriant and almost tropical character of its flora, takes the name of the "Golden shell." A quaint harmony of color, very pleasing to the eye, pervades the buildings, which are uniformly built, and it is this uniformity, perhaps, which served to throw the steeples and domes of the many sacred edifices into greater prominence. A public promenade called the Marina, somewhat elevated, skirts the bay; it is more than two hundred feet wide and is the most popular place of public resort. As seen from the ship on the afternoon of our arrival, this thoroughfare presented a most animated and pleasing scene. A constant stream of vehicles, presumably hauling the aristocracy of this beautiful Sicilian town, passed to and fro, while promenaders in great numbers strolled leisurely along. Away back in the distance above the surrounding hills, is seen Monreale or Mount Royal, which is celebrated for its church, said to be the handsomest in all Sicily.

A legend attaches to this church which claims that in the twelfth century, its founder, William the Good, who was hunting near this spot, fell asleep while resting, and had a vision, in which the Virgin commanded him to build a church on that ground.

Upon the return of the stewards next morning from their market trip, each, besides their baskets laden with the freshest and most delicious fruits, vegetables, and beautiful fish, brought glowing descriptions of the many attractions of which they had a glimpse during their brief interval ashore. C—— also informed me that he had been fortunate in securing the services of a young Sicilian who spoke English well and who would act as guide for us while here.

Louis and I went ashore after lunch and met the guide, Gætano Verduce, at the landing, and an hour later the casual observer would have put us down as life-long intimates.

He asked us to go with him to a neighboring café while he ate something, as he had not taken the time before for fear of missing us. The place was on the street floor in a very respectable looking house, situated on the Corso Vittorio Emmanuele, and I was surprised to find that nearly all of these otherwise imposing dwellings had this floor let for shop purposes. Gætano accompanied his repast with a bottle of wine, of which, upon his invitation, we partook, and found of pleasant taste. I was wondering how he could afford to drink wine with his lunch out of his earnings as guide, and my curiosity was satisfied a little later when he informed us that his lunch and wine had cost fifteen cents. Leaving here we took a carriage, as the weather was extremely warm, and besides we were anxious to see as much in a short while as possible.

The Corso Vittorio Emmanuele and the Corso Garibaldi, are the two principal streets, cutting each other at right angles near the city's center and leading to the four principal gates. The former extends from the Marina to the Royal palace, which marks the inner boundary of the city. The streets are generally well paved with lava blocks, and the two named, which are the scene of greatest activity during all hours, are kept quite clean. There are any number of small and irregular streets which run into these, and which are as filthy as the former are respectable. The houses are mostly flat roofed, with balconies projecting from one story or another, and the windows of these, closely shaded by Venetian blinds during the heated part of the day, are thrown wide in search of a refreshing evening breeze. We were first driven to the Cathedral, an imposing structure of the Arab-Norman style, built towards the end of the twelfth century; its original appearance has been carefully preserved, with the exception that during the present century a dome of fitting proportions has been added. The exterior of this edifice is elaborately ornamented, and we enter through a marble doorway, which is most beautifully carved. On a first view of the auditorium one is most strongly impressed with its loftiness, which effect is materially aided by several rows of pillars of finest granite, eighty in number, and which support the interior. Strange to say, the walls of this beautiful structure, rich with choice paintings, have been vulgarized by plain every-day whitewash. There is a statue of St. Rosalie, in honor of whom the 15th of July is set apart as the date of an annual pilgrimage in solemn procession to Monte Pelligrino, the scene of her death. It is said the bringing of her body to the cathedral caused an abatement of the plague, which was at that time raging in the city. Among the mausoleums, of which the cathedral contains quite a number, are to be seen those of Roger, the first of the Sicilian kings, and Frederick II; there are besides numerous sarcophaguses, in which are preserved the remains of several noted prelates.

We were next driven to the catacombs, situated in a large subterranean hall, over which is the convent of the Capuchins. We descended from the street into this ghoulish repository by means of a number of stone steps, and were met at the entrance by one of the monks of the order, who seemed to follow us about, possibly to prevent any acts of vandalism. The place is made up of numerous passages or compartments varying in size, in which these human relics appear in costume, the same as worn when living; the males standing and the females reclining in glass covered boxes. A label upon each body tells the name and date of birth and death. The clothing of some of the inmates of this charnel house, which was in some instances gay and flashy, furnished rather a comic feature to surroundings which were otherwise loathsomely dismal.

Young girls, whose cord of life had snapped in the sweet flush of youthful bloom, were simply clothed in a frock of purest white, while those of riper years had been arrayed in more pretentious toilets and rested now in grave and seeming conscious elegance, serenely indifferent to the lapse of years or Dame Fashion's many changes. Enclosed in tiny caskets lay the evidence of that unfathomed destiny, to which all nature must succumb; and there, in neighborly nearness, pitifully contrasted, stood those of sunken cheek and wrinkled brow. In a quiet corner, somewhat apart from the other silent ones, as though in tender respect for her sad story, had been placed the withered form of a young maiden. We were informed that within a few days of the time set for her marriage, her betrothed, who was returning from a long voyage, had been lost in a shipwreck; this misfortune was so great a shock as to unsettle her reason, and in the depth of her aberration and misery, she had ended her life by poison. She appeared clad in her bridal robes, with veil and wreath of orange blossoms on her brow.

Standing prominently in view was the body of an aged monk, clothed in the habiliments of the order.

While looking him over, we were admonished of the fact with much pride by one of the fraternity, that his tongue had been preserved, because he had never told a lie. His tag told us that he died in 1693. Our time was now very nearly exhausted, and we were nothing loth to leave behind these unwholesome sights and walk forth once more among living, breathing humanity.

On our next visit ashore Gætano took us to see several of the most noted churches, among them Santa Catherina, with its beautiful pavements in Florentine Mosaic and celebrated paintings; that of Martorana, a Norman structure of the twelfth century, its walls and splendid altar decorated with statues and flowers and rich with precious stones; the grand and beautiful San Domenico, with its massive gray columns and a seating capacity of more than ten thousand. Indeed, the visitor might profitably spend several days in viewing the rare beauty and lavish magnificence of these sacred edifices, many of which, besides the splendid display of mosaics, are prodigally adorned with lapis-lazuli, verd antique, malachite, and jasper.

Our afternoon was nearly spent before we realized it, and as it was now much pleasanter, we concluded to dismiss the conveyance and walk through the Corso Vittorio Emmanuele towards the Marina. This thoroughfare presented a very lively appearance, and in some respects reminded me of Chestnut street, Philadelphia, and were it not for the unknown musical tones which constantly greeted our ears, it would have been very easy to imagine ourselves on this popular street. Having occasion to do some shopping, we entered several stores and found business being pursued by much the same methods as in similar establishments across the water. The stores were large and well stocked with goods of all grades, and the gentlemen's furnishing store where we purchased collars and cuffs seemed to do also, in connection, a large business as a hatter. The window displays, especially of the jewelry stores, were tasteful and attractive. This walk, which with my companions was enjoyed very much, was in some respects a revelation as to the personal appearance of the Sicilians. In most large American cities the women are far ahead of the men in comeliness of feature, and a stroll out Connecticut avenue, Washington, offers a kaleidoscope of beauty and loveliness rarely equaled. The men, too, are quite good looking, at least they think they are; but Palermo, otherwise charming, has not bestowed upon her women that which Aristotle proclaimed to be better than all the letters of recommendation in the world, while to her men she has been more than generous.

At breakfast of the 22d, the Captain informed the steward that he would not be aboard for either lunch or dinner, and accorded us permission to spend the day ashore. As we were to sail on the morrow, we readily accepted, and together with Louis left the ship shortly after 12 o'clock.

We found Gætano, and after luncheon at the café "Neapolitaine," concluded to drive out to Villa Tasca, which with its beautiful park forms one of the places of interest to which strangers are directed. We were informed that Count Tasca, its owner, was an Italian nobleman of great wealth, who since the death of his wife had resided abroad.

We were soon rolling leisurely along the country road, which was pleasantly shaded, and passing now and again the simple country folk, who, under a temporary canvas shelter, were busily plying their looms or spinning wheels. We overtook several parties, the women in short skirts, which is their chief article of a costume, composed of many colors, carrying a bundle on the head, while the men trudged along with a burden slung to a staff over the shoulder. The road, being a gradual ascent of the mountain, afforded a delightful view of the surrounding country, as well as the harbor beyond with its many vessels lying gracefully at anchor. As we neared the gates of the park a keeper came out and drew the bolts, and, driving through, we entered a most perfect carriage way, which was found to skirt extensive fields, all of which were under one form or other of cultivation. We alighted at the entrance to the immediate enclosure of the castle, the walls of which were surmounted with skillfully wrought mural ornaments, and entered a smooth graveled walk, whose winding way threaded a labyrinth of rare plants, exhaling the most fragrant odors.

Making a slight detour we were ushered without warning into a delightfully cool underground passage extending perhaps fifty yards, whence we emerged to find at our feet a gurgling brook, running by the base of a hill, on the top of which stands a lofty palm, the reflection of whose broad leaves made an effective intermingling of sunshine and shadow on the surface of the narrow stream.

Leaving this pleasant prospect we shortly find ourselves on the bank of a miniature lake with its pleasure boat lying at the wharf of a most picturesque little boat-house.

This is a perfect little gem of artful construction, and its walls were almost covered with the names of visitors rudely carved, together with the date of inscription, and, upon the suggestion that it was possibly a good opportunity to place our names before a foreign public, we too inscribed.

We then ascended, by a series of irregular rustic steps, to a height of about a hundred feet. On the summit of this little hill was a charming little summer house, built of stone, its dome-like roof forming near the sides a succession of curves which descended to the base in the shape of pillars at a distance apart of three or four feet. The furniture of this inviting retreat was several iron chairs, deceiving one by their wood-like color and seeming delicate construction. While seated here in rapt admiration of these fairy-like domains, each busy with his own thoughts, time was speeding on, and of this fact we were made duly conscious when the hour for settling with the driver arrived. A keeper found us here and said that it wanted but a few minutes of six o'clock, at which time the gates would be closed for the night. Upon returning to town, Gætano pointed out to us the locality about which occurred, on March 30th, 1282, at the hour of vespers, the uprising and massacre which culminated in the expulsion of the French

ATTRACTIONS AT PALERMO AND MESSINA. 113

from the island, and known in history as "the Sicilian Vespers." It was after nine o'clock when we at last reached the landing and took leave of our friend and guide with mutual expressions of esteem and good wishes.

There being no ship's boat in, we hired a native to take us off, and in a little while were aboard ship and enjoying a welcome repose.

"All hands up anchor" sounding through the ship about two bells (one o'clock), on the afternoon of the 23d, and we know another pleasant visit is ended. The stewards went ashore as usual in the morning, but, seeing that we should only be one day out, there was nothing done in the way of provisioning more than ordinary marketing. About this time, when the crew were at their stations looking after the business in hand, an incident occurred which, while not on the program, was the occasion of some concern for at least one of the ship's company. The captain had luncheon early and was walking the poop deck while overlooking the progress in getting under way; the anchor had been catted and the men were walking away with the falls with a steady tramp, as the engines revolved and she moved towards the open sea. I was making some necessary arrangements in the cabin incident to leaving port, when loud and repeated calls came to my ears from towards the shore, and hastening to the cabin port, what was my astonishment to see our erstwhile guide and companion, Gætano, standing in a little boat gesticulating wildly, while being pulled towards the ship. When he had arrived under the stern he told the captain that one of the stewards owed him money which he had stood for as an accommodation in a transaction on shore. The captain immediately ordered the engines stopped and told him to come aboard, where he was met at the mast, and his complaint, which was against the ward-room steward, was formally heard. William was sent for and in reply said that he did owe the money but had not had the opportunity of getting it during the morning, and that he had intended sending it from Messina. The captain ordered the amount paid by the paymaster and charged to the steward's account, who was also rebuked. Gætano was profuse in his thanks as well as regrets for the delay occasioned, and as he went over the ship's side was followed by a generous outburst of applause from the sailors, who invariably love fair play and who had assembled in the gangway to watch results.

We were soon in motion once more and when outside, finding a good breeze, sail was made and the fires banked. We traveled along at an average of eight knots, our ship gallantly riding the long, graceful swells, with her full spread of canvas braced up to the wind, and the men in cool, white uniforms scattered here and there at work or play, and the whole forming a most pleasant picture of the poet's "sailing o'er a summer sea."

After dinner we filled our pipes and went forward for a walk and smoke. Everyone was wrapt in admiration for the beauties of the setting sun and the conditions generally which make a delightful evening at sea. There were a number of good voices aboard, and the call for a song was welcomed as a happy suggestion. C——, who was possessed of a very fine baritone, and Philip Rourke, an excellent tenor, with one or two others, were pressed into service and rendered several melodies in such manner as to draw about them the entire ship's company.

The impromptu concert was brought to a close just before eight bells (8 o'clock), with "Old Black Joe" and "Swanee River", in which all hands joined with hearty feeling and brought out of these old songs, so redolent of home and tender associations, a depth of pathos the effect of which was plainly visible. The captain with three of the ward-room officers sat down to a game of cribbage, shortly after eight bells, while C—— and I amused ourselves with a game of euchre in the pantry till past two bells (9 o'clock), when we prepared to turn in. Since leaving Gibraltar I had been sleeping on the berth deck, and, after reporting to the captain, we went forward and were soon in the restful embrace of our hammocks. It seemed I had only been asleep a short while, but in reality it was two bells, when I was awakened by the violent swinging of my hammock.

In the dim light of the berth deck, but partially awake, and seeing nearly three hundred hammocks describing a half circle, from some of which blankets hung and swept the deck in regular motion, I was completely bewildered. The situation was further aggravated by the noise made by the cups, pans, and kettles belonging to the berth deck cook playing hide-and-seek about the deck. It finally dawned upon me that the cabin must be in a fearful state of disorder, so I awakened C——, and after a hasty semi-toilet made our way aft. On entering the cabin a most ridiculous sight met our view, chairs and tables mounted on wheels engaged in a noisy steeple-chase, all over the room were strewn cards, pipes, and tobacco, and in the midst of all stood the captain in long night robe, hair disheveled, and looking generally like Lucifer deposed. The situation was too funny for restraint, and looking from one to the other we all burst into a hearty laugh. With much pitching and sliding we finally succeeded in restoring affairs to something like order, and after securing each piece of furniture and storing away all the movables, once more resigned ourselves to the influences of our restless hammocks. It is needless to add that we thoroughly appreciated the force of the lesson taught, viz.: that beneath the surface of the calmest waters often lurks the fury of the tempest, as well as in social life the dispassionate eye and unruffled brow often surmount a soul melting with the fervent heat of criminal impulse and shameful vice.

When we came on deck at two bells (5 o'clock), on the morning of the 24th, every sign of the recent roughness had disappeared, and, instead of the stiff breeze that had filled our sails, we found an almost perfect calm.

Sail had been taken in during the mid-watch and the vessel put under steam. We again came in sight of the coast of Sicily about two bells (9 o'clock), and shortly before noon were anchored in the harbor of Messina.

This harbor, which is also strongly fortified, is

counted among the finest in the world. There were several war vessels in, and the commercial importance of the place was fully attested by the vast amount of shipping which lined the wharves and stretched out along the entire front of the city. As seen from the ship it is difficult to imagine a city more picturesquely beautiful, forming as it does an amphitheatre of well-built structures of white stone clearly defined against a background of luxuriant verdant hills.

The principal street extends along the water front, and throughout its length have been built splendid buildings, while a number of churches, highly ornamental in design, have been interspersed and lend a most pleasing feature. Messina is not so attractive to the sightseer as its larger sister Palermo, and among its objects of especial interest the cathedral perhaps ranks first. It was built in the 12th century and partly destroyed by the earthquake of 1783. Designed after the Gothic it impresses the beholder as dark and gloomy, which effect is only felt on the outside, however, for, upon entering, the eye, having become accustomed to the soft light, sees everywhere the evidences of the highest art as well as lavish richness.

The pulpit is of marble and handsomely carved, while mosaics and precious stones have been used with great effect for purposes of adornment.

Enormous granite columns is another feature which contributes in no small degree to the beauty and grandeur of the whole.

Among the relics of which the city boasts is one purported to be an autograph letter of the Holy Virgin, testifying to her appreciation of the Messinians and assuring them of her constant care and support.

In proof of this they point with pride to the fact that an abundance of corn was sent to them at a time when famine was abroad in the land. The evening of our arrival the Captain, with the American consul, attended the opera, and at breakfast next morning said it was something we should not on any account miss.

We left the ship after lunch for the day as the Captain had an engagement to dine ashore, and were soon doing the city in a very modest though comfortable conveyance. We drove a considerable distance beyond, through a country rich and fertile, where the golden fruit which has become famous in the principal markets of the world, weighted down the parent stem or, through very ripeness having lost its adhesive force, lay waiting for the gatherer.

Returning to town we had an excellent dinner at the Victoria, and at the proper time repaired to the opera house. My idea of such a place was of course in accord with what I know of such institutions in America; we were, therefore, very much surprised after passing the main entrance, to be ushered through into an apartment about the size of the usual theatre box. These we noticed were of uniform size and rose to the height of six or seven tiers overlooking the pit, in the center of which was a fountain, the play of whose bright, sparkling water fell with refreshing pleasure on the senses.

The odd structure was entirely roofless save for the bejeweled vault of a summer sky. The stage, which was of good size, screened its mysteries behind a curtain of rich design and beauty, while over the whole there floated an air of romance in which the subdued murmur of voices, whose owners were unseen, mingled in delicate harmony with the splash and fall of the waters of the fountain.

The performance itself was pleasing and from an operatic standpoint left nothing to be desired. To be sure, we had to depend entirely upon the pantomine for an interpretation of the sentiment, for the programs may as well have been blank as far as we were concerned. The evening was withal thoroughly enjoyable, and at the conclusion of the play we were no less interested in watching the merry throng of gaily dressed ladies and their escorts as they came forth into the calm beauty of the summer night.

Our stay here was somewhat longer than the captain had intended, as he decided to give the men twenty-four hours' liberty, which seemed to have been thoroughly appreciated, for all hands showed up at the proper time and in good condition.

We left Messina at 10 A. M., the 28th of June, bound for Port Said, generously supplied with delicious fruits and an abundance of other provisions, calculated to contribute in no small degree to the pleasures of a six days' trip at sea. The weather was different from any we had so far experienced. A thick haze enveloped the surrounding country and hung like a pall over the harbor, as we steamed out into the open sea.

The men broke out their oil-skins and sea-boots,

and preparations were made generally for a spell of bad weather.

About noon the lookout reported a sail on our port bow; she was made out one of the P. & O. passenger steamers and appeared to be making a course from one of the north Mediterranean ports and heading for the canal.

Our experience on this the first day out from Messina was such as to require everyone to hunt up his sea legs, which may have been thrown aside during the previous pleasant weather, for the *Ossipee* had gotten on a decidedly hilarious jag, and with the aid of a high rolling sea was as well contented to go sideways as ahead.

This tendency was of course unpleasant to everyone, but most of us who may have been forced to maintain as nearly as possible a vacuum, during the first days of our sailor life, had since become in this respect at least the veriest old salts and could now boast an anatomy to which upheavals were strange and unknown.

There was one of the ship's company, however, who was made of delicate stuff, Cody of the marine guard, and to him the sympathy of all hands was extended. Since leaving Philadelphia he had ever been prey for the monster sea-sickness, and on each occasion that we left port poor Cody was called upon to "stand and deliver," and he was very brave, he never seemed to tire, and although the summons often came when on duty, he would simply step aside to the waist and in a little while return proudly, though tearfully, to the scene of action. Towards evening on the 29th, we noticed with pleasure signs of clear weather, and when we came on deck next morning old Nepture seemed smiling an apology for his recent frowns and bad temper, which our good ship gracefully acknowledged by shaking out her sails and standing away on her course at an increased speed.

Punctually on schedule time the sun appeared above the western horizon on the morning of the 4th of July, casting aslant the broad waters a dazzling sheen of sparkling radiance and mounted in a chariot of fire to his appointed course.

The day was observed as a holiday, and aside from the usual early morning work of "washing down," all routine was suspended. The men were called to quarters at nine o'clock, after which awnings were spread fore and aft, under which the crew employed themselves with some form of personal industry or amusement.

The sun beamed intensely hot, and in the light of past experience one could easily imagine the thousands of sweltering beings in the States in gay holiday dress, retreating to one or another of the shady parks or groves or embarking to spend the day where nature holds perpetual charm, on the shores of the grand old ocean and in the music of its roar. A refreshing breeze stirred under our awnings, and officers and men, although apparently exiled, seemed to account for naught both time and space, and share with zeal feelings of pride and exultation on this anniversary of American liberty.

The ward-room officers kept the day by an elaborate dinner, at which the Captain was the honored guest, and a merry tinkle of glass, responsive to toasts of patriotism, mingled with laughter and applause, fully attested the pleasure of the occasion. With cordial generosity and good feeling the men were not permitted to be forgotten, and to each division was sent, with the compliments of its officer, a generous contribution of wine, beer, or cigars. An evening of singing and story-telling on the foc'sle brought to a close a pleasant day, and early on the morning of the 5th we anchored in the bay of Port Said.

CHAPTER VIII.

THROUGH THE SUEZ CANAL.

WE have come at length, fellow voyagers, to the very portal of the fabulous East, and pause before entering its ancient territory for a brief survey of this little city whose inhabitants bow before the crescent and look to Mohammed as the source of their inspiration and worship.

Port Said may be considered the peculiar offspring of the Suez Canal, and to have had its origin in the necessity for a basis of operations at the European or western end of that gigantic undertaking.

A magnificent light-house, attaining an elevation of one hundred and sixty feet, the flash of whose electric light is plainly visible more than twenty miles away, stands an enduring monument to the untiring zeal exhibited in this great enterprise.

It is built of blocks of concrete of like substance as those which form the mole which skirts the harbor. These blocks are said to be composed of seven parts of desert sand and one of French hydraulic lime so skillfully worked as to produce an artificial stone of wonderful strength and beauty. The great harbor has been constructed at immense expense, and no labor has been thought too great to complete and perfect this, the northern entrance to the canal.

Ton after ton of matter had to be dredged out to make the basin of sufficient depth, while to preserve the progress made by this means and to prevent additional deposits of sediment, two enormous dams of stone were built running parallel far out into the sea.

At the beginning of the canal in 1859, the village embraced only a few native huts; but the magic touch of enterprise and genius soon lent their developing influences, and at its completion, ten years later, there had grown on these hot sands a city of an estimated population of nearly twenty thousand.

There is a European and Arab settlement. La Cannebiere is the principal street of the former, and along this are found the largest buildings in which the different navigation companies and various government offices make their homes. They have a solid appearance and are usually of two stories, each having a broad veranda built about it, where the people of the house, who utilize the upper story for dwelling purposes, may be seen at all hours of the day or night lounging, smoking, and talking. The doors of some of the more substantial looking houses have been handsomely carved and have ancient looking iron knockers and wooden locks. Several were also adorned with inscriptions in Arabic.

All Egyptian streets are very narrow, designedly so, as preventing a greater diffusion of the sun's rays, and thereby contributing somewhat to the general comfort. In the business street in front of the little pens, the largest not more than six feet square, in which the dealers employ themselves as workers in metals or venders of curios, have been suspended rudely constructed awnings, which furnish a grateful shade and invite the wayfarer to linger and perchance to purchase as well as gossip. Now and again a train of camels, with their swaying, billowy motion, make their noiseless way through the street and by their presence complete most effectually a picture, the outlines of which have been more or less defined in the mind of every reader.

On the evening of July 5th, Louis and I went ashore and after roaming around aimlessly for more than an hour stopped at the "Concordia," a public house, where my companion made the acquaintance of a young German who volunteered his services as guide. We first visited the site of the old Arab settlement which had been destroyed by fire two years previously, leaving only heaps of charred and blackened ruins. The new village, which was located nearer the seaboard, consisted of a net-work of little huts stretched out along the coast for more than a mile. At the time of our visit, the evening meal was in progress, and as we sauntered in and out among the tents we became familiar with several features of the domestic economy. The food, which was dished from a large iron pot swung from a tripod before each tent, had the appearance of dirty rice, which they ate with their fingers while squatting about. A semi-serious expression on their faces was usually replaced by one of amusement as we came in view.

There was quite a number of tents fitted up as saloons, each of which was generously patronized by dirty looking Arabs sitting about smoking and drinking. Further along we came to a portion of the settlement in which only women seemed to dwell, and at sight of our little procession they ran out of their tents gesticulating wildly, while several of the number, without regard for the flimsy texture of the one piece which composed their costume, performed various antics with an abandon of wantonness that soon reduced us to flight. This act seemed to please them immensely, as two or three, encouraged by the others, gave chase. We had proceeded but a short way when Louis lost his cap, which one of the women overhauled and ran, waving it aloft, back to the tent. After vainly trying for more than an hour to regain the cap we were at length obliged to appeal to the native police, who after alternate threatenings and pleadings were finally successful in restoring it to us.

On the occasion of another visit ashore, which was made after dinner was over aboard ship, we visited several "Café Chantants," in which orchestras of Vienna female musicians were the popular attractions. A portion of our ship's company was on liberty, and in consequence the few resorts in which exhilarating fluids were to be had did a rushing business. The most popular of these places seemed to be the Concordia, and we had scarcely entered before several of the boys were around us insisting on our joining them in a friendly glass.

The beverage most indulged in was English beer, which sold for a shilling a bottle.

Numerous small tables were placed about the

large room, which had a platform at one end for the musicians, and around these the company, embracing representatives of several nations, were seated.

The tables were served by European waiters in black jackets, whom we learned were compensated at the rate of one dollar per day and board.

At the conclusion of each piece the orchestra were permitted to recreate among the audience, and incidently to accept sundry invitations to "imbibe the amber," at the expense of willing admirers. We remained interesting spectators for some little while of this very lively scene, and after standing our treat with the boys started forth in search of other sights. We next looked in at a large café kept by a German called "The Bismarck." The daughter of the proprietor, a very charming girl of about seventeen, performed the duties of waitress, and it was readily apparent that she was the presiding genius of the establishment, and ruled her loving parent as completely as did she the shaggy little pet which trotted about her heels or challenged her notice by pulling playfully at her dress.

We ordered a light lunch, and while it was being prepared mine host, who spoke English, entertained us with some of his experiences during the twelve years he had made Port Said his home. The little waitress in a short while brought our order, and, strange to say, in her presence, food seemed a secondary consideration, for each was eager to engage her in conversation. The pleasure, however, fell to Louis, for he was her countryman and addressed her in German, in which she with evident pleasure responded, and from then until we left he worked the monopoly to his entire satisfaction and enjoyment.

It was about 9.30 when we left the café and decided to walk around awhile before returning to the ship.

The night was beautiful in the extreme; the moon, the peerless gem in nature's star-decked dome, was never more radiantly brilliant, and when we had gotten beyond the more thickly-settled locality, a full and powerful sense of the sublimity of this unusual scene completely filled me. It is easy and natural in such surroundings to recall some of the interesting history which, with their impressively sacred associations, cluster about this Egypt-land, and which in many respects form the pillars upon which rest the Christian belief. I found myself in the country in which Joseph and the Virgin and the child Jesus sojourned during their memorable flight, where they drank from a sweet stream of purest water, so changed from the impure and muddy fountain source by the especial care of the invisible hand which guided them. Here the child Moses, doomed with those of his age and race to an early death by the cruel hatred of a powerful ruler, was found in the bulrushes by the tender daughter of an unnatural parent, and taken to her heart and home to become in later years the especial law-giver of the Christian church.

Look with me over these broad sands, think on the countless millions of nature's men who have lived their day, founded ancient cities, achieved an old world fame in the arts of peace and war, and one by one have gone to take their places in the "silent halls." Greater truth was never uttered than: "*We built with what we call eternal rock; a distant age asks where the fabric stood, and in the dust sifted and searched in vain the undiscoverable secret sleeps.*"

Behold here, also, a land wherein has been wrought a history more strange than the weirdest fiction, the land of the world's greatest builders, to whom the pyramids of Cheops, Dashur, and Sahara, with their unmistakable evidences of original skill, attest in silent tones the wonderful resources of these primitive workers.

Think on the Colossus of Rameses and the grand old Sphinx, which with the accumulated calm of the ages overlooks the sweep of mortality with a supreme and awful indifference:

"That Heavenly monarch who his foes defies,
Like Vulcan powerful and like Pallas wise."

It was now ten o'clock, and as we drew leisurely nearer the Arab quarters our ears caught the sound of native music, in which mingled the voices of men and women tuned in doubtful melody to the measures of the strain.

Quickening our pace in the hope of witnessing some unusual ceremony, we were soon repaid with the view of a most extraordinary scene.

There were assembled on the outskirts of the tented village, on the side towards the sea, a crowd of young and old and of both sexes, numbering several hundred.

A large circular place about which the dusky

crowd stood or moved around was given up to several musicians and one dancer, a young Arab woman. She wore a short skirt of delicate muslin of generous fold which reached to the knee; a vest of bright colors, tightly fitting, formed an artistic covering for the upper portion of her body, while a loose undergarment of the same texture as the skirt peeped from beneath this and hung in graceful fullness about the waist.

Her form, which showed a wonderful muscular development, was plentifully adorned with massive ornaments of both gold and silver.

Above her bare feet she wore anklets of gold, and on her arms, which disclaimed all other covering, shone bangles of native coins.

Hoops of silver hung from her ears and a plaited band of the same metal with comb attached confined, in a loose though graceful coil, the lustrous black hair at the back of her shapely head. She was scarcely more than twenty; the exercise had caused a delicate flush to glow in her nut-brown cheek, while in the fringed depths of her great dark eyes there sparkled the evidence of mischievous delight.

She seemed to notice nothing or no one, but with lips half parted in a languorous smile, slightly disclosing her pearl white teeth, she interpreted by the rhythm of motion the subtle charm of the native Arab dance.

A score or more flaming torches held aloft by onlookers made a flickering circle over the heads of the outer rim of spectators, reflecting in a half tone the faces of those within its rays and contrasting weirdly with the mellow flood of moonlight cast over all.

Pressing forward with true American persistence, we soon reached the inner circle and took a stand within a few feet of the dancer.

The various stages of the performance, which seemed to take their cue from the turn of the music, reflected the changing feelings and emotions of the performer, and might be termed an epic in individual action or a story told in motion.

A rapid and vigorous muscular contortion in exact and even time with the now rasping tones of the music would be gradually relieved by a quivering tremulousness, during which her whole upper frame would be shaken as with the ague and every thrill of motion would correspond, in time and degree, to the rhythm of ever-changing music. The muscular effort by which the perfection of the dance or the skill of the performer is apparently judged, is simply wonderful.

The even tension and control which enable the performer to represent, in this voiceless language of muscle and motion, a variety of moods and feelings, may only be witnessed in this extraordinary dance. At a peculiar and sudden turn in the music, which becomes more suggestively languorous, the responsive motion of the performer became extremely indelicate and shocking.

The effect of this unusual play upon the native spectators was intensely interesting to the casual observer. After an occasional outburst of wordy applause, relieving their overwrought sensibilities and expressive of unrestrained admiration, they would subside into a mood of calm and contemplative regard, during which their pleasure evinced itself by a sympathetic movement of head and body, while a smile of ardent though quiet delight illumined each swarthy countenance.

The morning of July 9th, our last day in port, was passed taking on and storing away provisions, the usual preparations for sea being omitted in view of the two days of easy travel before us while passing through the canal. At noon of this day, the Jews, who are the principal dealers, came aboard with their stock of curios, consisting of paper cutters and weights, jewel and toilet boxes made of wood from the Holy Land, specimens of flowers from Gethsemane and Jerusalem mounted on cards, bottles of attar of roses, old native coins, jewelry of pearl, gold and silver, etc. An Egyptian juggler bewildered quite a number of the officers and men by various sleight-of-hand tricks; one of these particularly remembered as creating a great deal of interest was performed with the aid of a pair of snow-white rabbits. A turban of soft creamy stuff, deftly wound about his head with many folds, o'ershadowed a pair of shaggy brows beneath which his small cold brown eyes shone forth with a snap and sparkle rarely met with in a race so well known for cupidity and native cunning.

His face, unusually tanned by exposure, was of a delicate brown, and offered a decided contrast to his breast, several shades lighter, a glimpse of which was had beneath his half-open shirt. Seated tailor style on the deck with his craftsman's tools exposed on a cloth before him, he took a rabbit in each hand and slowly rubbed them one against the other, mumbling in a crooning tone all the while; in less than a minute one of the little pets had disappeared and the one remaining, being released, went hopping about the deck. Everyone thought, although we had watched him closely, that he had in some way secreted the missing one within the folds of his voluminous garment, but the most careful search, undertaken by one of the officers on his invitation, failed to produce the missing article. By a like process of rubbing and devil talking (as one of the men expressed it), number two was brought in evidence and, after taking a collection he left us completely mystified; and while unbelieving still conceding him a mastery of the black art, more confusing than is attained by the average performer.

At 5 A. M. on the 10th, we were under way through the Suez Canal; the king of day, already leaving his eastern couch clothed in robes of fire, had serenely mounted to his dazzling course, diffusing rays of ever-increasing heat, until as early as nine o'clock the thermometer showed a register of 96 degrees. The regulation quarters and drills were dispensed with and the order was passed for all hands to make themselves comfortable in whatever dress responded to the individual idea.

The men soon appeared in various go-as-you-please costumes, in which "tights" seemed to be the favorite, with a blouse and trousers of white duck, the legs well rolled up and sleeves cut out, a close second. Bared feet was the prevailing fashion, and as the decks were frequently watered a degree of comfort was found through these means adopted at the kindly instance of the Captain, and was thoroughly appreciated by all on board.

No work of any kind was undertaken except that made necessary by the pilot's orders in working the ship. The regulations of the Canal Company prohibit vessels from attaining a greater speed than five miles an hour, thus in a measure freeing from liability to accident the many vessels of all sizes which make use of its franchise. The width of the canal varies from two to three hundred feet at the surface and is of a mean width of seventy-five feet at the bottom. It is a hundred miles long, three-fourths of which is actual canal, the remaining one-fourth being comprised in the lakes and small islands which abound near its center.

The history of the several efforts to establish communication by means of canal between one or another of three great highways of traffic, which are the redeeming features of this otherwise barren section, are most interesting and unmistakably attest the resourceful genius of the ancients, in no less degree than the matchless sagacity and determined zeal of modern minds.

The first undertaking by which it was sought to join a branch of the Nile and the Red Sea, was probably about 1300 B. C., and at various intervals throughout the years which have elapsed the mind of man has been exercised in this direction, while to the present century must be accredited the great Suez Canal, worthily ranking among the most splendid and solid achievements of man in any age.

We watched the glistening sands stretch out from

either bank showing no sign of grass or shrub, drearily the same and unbroken by hill or vale. Thus Asia and Africa, so long wedded topographically as well as in the moral and social sense, being now divorced by this narrow strip of water and by it brought in constant communication with a steady stream of civilizing influences, is it not reasonable to hope that the long night of darkness and superstition which has hung as a pall over the latter land may be indeed far spent and the dawn of a glorious civilization almost at hand?

At noon while the hands were at dinner, our attention was drawn to the African bank by a series of unusual sounds which caused a general rush to the forecastle; a hearty laugh was enjoyed upon finding a jolly band of eight or ten Arab youngsters, girls and boys, clad only in nature's simple dress, trotting along the edge of the bank. Our little escorts soon made known that they were not having their hide scorched purely for pastime, but that they were out for the "stuff," and ready and willing to pick up anything we might throw them. The men tossed them a lot of broken hard-tack and other remnants from their dinner which caused a lively scramble and with which they soon disappeared.

About three o'clock the pilot ran us into one of the little slips which was conveniently provided at intervals along the canal, and by the use of which a vessel coming from an opposite direction is enabled to pass.

An hour later the peninsular and oriental steamer *Calcutta*, carrying Her Majesty's mail, steamed slowly past us. At seven o'clock we anchored off the little town of Ismailia.

A boat was called away to take a few of the officers and the cabin steward ashore, all of whom were required to be aboard at eleven o'clock, so that there would be no delay in getting under way next morning.

A few of the men went to the "mast" and secured permission for the crew to go in swimming. The dingey was called away as a rescuer in case of accident to any of the bathers and speedy preparations were made for a refreshing plunge. The forward-port torpedo-boom was "rigged-out" with rope ladder suspended, which, together with the port gangway, afforded ample accommodations for the more modest and less venturesome divers.

A few experts gave a graceful exhibition in diving and jumping from the fore-yard arm and were heartily applauded by onlookers.

Various aquatic feats were performed and contests of skill and endurance engaged in with much spirit and enjoyment.

At the end of half an hour the boatswain's call put an end to the evening's frolic, and there clambered aboard a set of men whom a special or unlooked-for privilege could not have pleased half so well as the granting of this simple and innocent amusement.

Our second day in the canal was not unlike the first. Passed through Bitter Lake shortly after noon and at seven in the evening came to an anchorage in the Gulf of Suez.

At five o'clock next morning all hands were called,

the market boat sent ashore, and the usual preparations made for going to sea.

The city of Suez, as viewed from the ship, had the appearance of being solidly built and presented a strong contrast to the mere fishing village it was reported to have been a little more than twenty years ago. The various storehouses of the steamship companies are imposing structures; as also the English hospital, while the Chalet of the Khedive, a noble edifice situated on an eminence commanding a glorious view of city and harbor, challenges favorable comparison with the more famous palaces of the rulers of other lands. A few of the officers went ashore at eight o'clock and returned at twelve. The captain, who had been suffering from an attack of rheumatic gout, remained aboard.

At luncheon he said we would get under way at two o'clock, and by keeping a sharp lookout we might, if the atmosphere was sufficiently clear, be rewarded during the afternoon by a view of the Sinai group. About four o'clock, with the aid of the ship's glasses, we sighted them far away in the hazy distance, their historic peaks lost in mist and cloud, leaving their lower outline, indistinctly visible, rising in irregular forms from out the sandy plain.

No unusual occurrence was recorded during the passage through the Red Sea. We followed the course adopted by large vessels, keeping well to the middle channel, thereby avoiding the many submerged islands, coral reefs, and shoals which are a menace to navigation.

We found the weather but slightly different from

that encountered in the canal. The day's duties performed in a perfunctory manner brought us to a night of restless discomfort. Whatever breeze there was came to us from the hot sands of the desert and was as refreshing to the person as would be a draught from the drying-room of a modern laundry. The only really enjoyable part of the twenty-four hours was in the early morning when the usual holy-stoning and washing down of decks was in progress.

It was delightful then to feel the caressing coolness of the water as we splashed about in our bare feet or took our turn as a target to be played upon by an invigorating stream from the hose.

A ludicrous scene was furnished each night when a number of the men, routed out by the insufferable heat of the berth deck, would come up through the hatchways, bringing their mattress and blanket, seeking a breath of air and literally realizing the sacred injunction, "Take up thy bed and walk." During these nights the forecastle became a veritable lodging house, and here poor Jack would roll to and fro, with the motion of the ship, till, roused by the boatswain's call, he would pull his aching bones together and take up the duties of another day.

We passed the Straits of Bab-el-Mandeb in the night of July 18th, and at eleven o'clock on the morning of the 19th, cast anchor in the Gulf of Aden.

The initial phase of Asiatic life presented to our notice was extremely amusing and afforded enjoyable diversion to both officers and men.

A host of little dark brown boys paddled out to the ship in canoes, formed from the burnt out trunk of a tree, and gave an exhibition of their proficiency in diving.

They were from ten to fourteen years of age and entirely free from clothing except a small cloth about the loins. Their hair, perhaps originally black, was curly and of a decided reddish tinge, presumably made so by constant contact with salt water, which had also effected a similar change in the whites of their small, restless eyes.

Our attention was first drawn to them by a strange and not altogether unmusical chorus formed of the words "Yes, sar! throw away! I dive! I dive! throw away! throw away!" This brought a substantial response in the way of small coin, and immediately paddles were dropped in the boat and over the little fellows would go into the water. Some remained beneath the surface a marvelously long time, and on re-appearing would first hold the coin aloft, and then strike out rapidly for their canoe which would be drifting slowly away.

Aden, which was taken by the British early in the present century, is sometimes known as the "Gibraltar of the Red Sea."

It is fortified by a garrison of English troops, and from position and natural advantages is considered a stronghold, but slightly inferior to its namesake of the Mediterranean.

It is built on a rocky projection which stretches out into a narrow strip, by which it is joined to the mainland of Arabia.

The inhospitable naked heights with dwellings meagerly scattered here and there, furnish a most uninviting prospect. The barren character of the sandy soil and infrequent signs of vegetation, upon which the sun seems to shine with unwonted vigor, produces a most unfavorable impression upon the traveler. It is said, however, that numerous plantations and gardens highly cultivated abound in a section invisible from the port.

Coffee is extensively grown and is exported in large quantities.

Possessing a magnificent port, Aden has become an important factor in the increasing traffic between India and Africa, and affords a most convenient station for supplies of coal and other articles.

A population of between thirty and forty thousand is composed of the different branches derived from Arabian stock, with a fair contingent of Somalis, Abyssinians, Negroes, and Jews. We remained here five days, during which coal was taken on and general preparations made for the trip across the Indian ocean.

A most agreeable surprise was afforded me when the master-at-arms, who was distributing the mail to the assembled crew, passed me three letters, two from home and one from my friend H———. These furnished me the first news I had received since the cruise began. I was delighted to find one of them from my father and the other from cousin Bob. Through these I was informed of many interesting occurrences, mostly of a pleasant nature. The ward-room steward joined us in the pantry in the evening and through contributions from each an interesting *pot pourri* of news was formed which kept us till long after midnight. C—— was greatly disappointed at not receiving a letter he had looked for from Washington, but, with his usual jovial spirit, seemed speedily to forget the disappointment and became a delighted partaker of the little feast. Friend H——'s letter, which was the next topic of interest, proved a source of gratification to the eager listeners and read as follows :

"June 29, 1884.

"Dear John :

"I was very glad to receive your letter last night. It arrived here six days before me, and served the purpose of a messenger to my people.

"In the letter which you posted for me at Gibraltar, I informed my parents of my intention of leaving the ship at the earliest opportunity, in consequence of which, they have been worrying themselves more than was necessary.

"When your letter arrived, they, under the influence of great anxiety and suspense, lost all fear of my indignation (if I should feel any) and opened the letter, which afforded them great relief and not a little amusement; relief, because from what you had stated, and the fact that you had written from Palermo, they felt convinced that I was safe and on my way homeward, and amusement, caused by your happy and graphic description of a rough night at sea, and the ludicrous appearance of the Captain as described by you. I must confess you are robbing the literary world of a great treasure in going to sea. I don't what you think about. Well, old fellow, after I had parted from you that last night at "Gib" I went to bed and slept soundly till half-past four the next morning, when I got up, washed and dressed and prepared for two or three days (as I knew it to be) hard work: well, after partaking of what little food I had, I started from the hotel and boldly walked out of the town, through the gates, across the English and Spanish lines into "Elina." When I arrived in Spanish Town, I felt and breathed a little easier; although not perfectly safe, I knew I was on the right road to getting safely away. After passing through Elina, I followed the road to San Roque, where I rested some little time, and from thence across some great hills and a sandy plain, and found myself about noon on the margin of a forest of cork-yielding trees, which I was compelled to traverse to get to a place called "Pablo." I at once plunged into the forest, not knowing whether I was going right or wrong, but all the same going straight ahead; when I had been walking about a couple of hours, I came to a little hut on a clear space surrounded by trees, and there I rested myself and partook of some refreshments, provided by the lady of the house.

"While resting at the hut a party of muleteers and their teams were going by, and on being asked by the lady of the house whither they were going, answered "To Malaga;" when I heard "To Malaga," my heart gave a great bound, and I felt overcome with joy; it seemed to me a special act of Providence, the sending of these men in my way, and I fervently thanked God for my deliverance from I knew not what, but, I knew that about eighty miles of mountainous country lay between me and my destination, and I knew not a foot of the way, and here were guides (it seemed to me especially sent), ready and willing for the sake of my company, to conduct me.

"I hastily finished and paid for my repast, and started on the road with my newly-found friends and guides, and after about six hours hard traveling, up hill and down hill, rough road and smooth road, but with an astonishingly small percentage of smooth road, we at last reached "Pablo," where we rested for the night. To make a long story short, I must tell you we had four days hard traveling, making about twenty miles a day over mountains and hills, with a river here and there, which I found to be very hard work, and which I should not like to go through again. Well we arrived at last, safely at "Malaga," where I at once went in search of an English ship, and was fortunate enough to find one bound for London, the day after my arrival in Malaga; I found the Captain aboard and made terms with him, in which transaction it was agreed between us that I should hand over my watch and chain to the ship's steward for safe keeping, as a pledge of my good intention to pay him (the Captain) a certain sum of money claimed by him, for my keep while aboard his ship, and which I was to redeem on my arrival in London; so I got aboard next day and joyfully started (*en route*) for England, which we reached after fifteen days sail. The reason we were so long on the journey, is that we were aboard a freight boat and had to call at Cadiz, Lisbon, and Vigo, but I did not care about the time, knowing that I was bound for England, and safe away from Gibraltar.

"My people, I need not tell you, were overjoyed to see me once more, and I have had to relate every incident of my life while aboard the *Ossipee* to them, and many friends besides, so I assure you your name has been mentioned more than once.

. . . .

"Remember me to my good friend Cary, and bespeaking for you a most prosperous cruise, and trusting the pleasure of welcoming you to dear old England may be mine at some future day, I remain,

"Your devoted friend,

"H——."

We were in no way regretful when the time came to pick up anchor, for this being deemed an unfitting place in which to grant liberty, the crew were anxious to reach Colombo and have a run ashore.

The Captain spoke in terms the most complimentary of the hospitality accorded him by the American Consul and several English residents, and before leaving the former sent aboard for the ship's company several large sacks of Mocha coffee, which was gratefully enjoyed by all.

At eight o'clock on the morning of the 24th, we steamed away towards the sweet-scented island of Ceylon.

Scarcely had we left the Gulf of Aden, ere there was noticeable a very great change in the weather.

We found the sea rough and choppy, and the atmosphere delightfully cool and refreshing, which was in the nature of a blessing after the recent torrid experiences in the canal and Red Sea.

Life seemed indeed now worth living; each day

brought to our notice some of the many interesting forms of life with which the mighty deep abounds.

The rapid changing combinations of fleeting clouds in which might be traced the most fantastic shapes and images, grotesque and otherwise, were eagerly watched from hour to hour and furnished a beautiful topic for speculation and amusement.

The mornings were invariably bright and clear until towards noon, when the clouds began to gather, sometimes black and threatening, and again light and fleecy, changing ever, a wondrous panorama suspended 'twixt sea and sky, the majesty of space pervading all, solemn, grand, interminable.

A strong and favoring wind, which caught us on leaving Aden, lasted during the greater part of the trip and gave us a daily average of about eleven knots per hour.

The *Ossipee*, as usual, in a heavy sea, pitched and rolled a great deal, in consequence of which there was considerable distress among the sea-sick "regulars."

An occasional heavy squall, during which the wind blew a gale and the sea with every roll swept furiously across the deck, brought all hands to their stations, to shorten or take in sail, after which the usual routine would be resumed.

The island of Ceylon was sighted early on the morning of August 4th, and at nine o'clock we were buoyed within its magnificent breakwater.

This is more than a mile in length, and, as the name implies, effectively breaks the force of the outer sea and affords a safe and convenient harbor for vessels of considerable size.

The sea, dashing furiously against this line of rock along its entire length, would shoot high in the air forming at unequal distances a series of fantastic shapes and figures; now developing a huge shaft or pyramid, and again ascending in a delicate column and spreading as it went its force in a shower of silvery gems. At night, when the moon lent lustre to the scene, the effect was most impressive, and buoyed within fifteen or twenty yards we were often sensibly affected by a heavy spray or enveloped in clouds of mist.

The island of Ceylon, which was held at different periods by the Portuguese and Dutch, has been possessed by the English since 1795.

Of its larger cities, Colombo has in late years grown to be the most important, and has, through affording more convenient portage for vessels plying the Indian trade, managed to gradually divert much of the traffic from its neighbor, Point de Galle, notwithstanding the advantage of an excellent deep-water harbor enjoyed by the latter.

The effect of British brains, energy, and wealth, are everywhere seen. Splendid roads are maintained throughout the island.

The government controls the railroads, telegraph, and a major part of the banking business; though an exchange business, involving considerable capital, is successfully carried on between native merchants of Bombay and the island.

A fort, well garrisoned by English soldiers, is not

the least among the influences which invite native respect and confidence. The sea touches this on two sides, and the rocky eminence upon which it is built is connected with the mainland by a large lake which is spanned by several bridges. The fort is laid off in narrow streets, in which are found the offices and business houses of European merchants. The governor's residence, styled the "Queen's House," is the most prominent of the several public buildings.

The barracks in which the troops are housed are large comfortable structures, situated along the water at the south front of the fort; near these is the military hospital, and stretching out from here is the common known as "Galle Face." There may be seen upon this beautiful green, on any evening during the season, a living picture full of color and beauty, and presenting all the lights and shades of fashionable life; a sort of social airing place, such as Central Park, New York, differing only in fact that many of those here seen on the foremost crest of the social swim, though decidedly *off color*, are in no sense *de trop*, as their cousins of various tints would be considered if seen in any numbers in the last-named resort.

A person traveling from place to place, either by land or water, becomes by contrast more or less familiar with the distinctive features which attain in the local routine or economy. The watchful eye will also notice various changes, often retrograde, sometimes progressive, in the construction, fitting, or adaptation of one or another of the means employed in the trade of large ports or cities.

This idea is strangely exemplified when a review is made of the various styles of boats in use by native people at the different ports visited, for purpose of carriage or traffic between shore and ship.

Here at Colombo the example which gave shape to this idea was most striking and peculiar. The hollowed-out trunk of a tree about eighteen or twenty feet long, with an average width of less than two feet, formed the body of the boat. The sides, elevated a foot or more by well-seasoned boards, forms the support for an out-rigger of stout bamboo cane, which touches the surface of the water on a line parallel to itself. This is connected by two curved bamboo canes of smaller size placed in a position at right angles to either end.

A sail made from the fibre of the palm is skillfully adjusted and handled with consummate ease and daring. In these little vessels, which at first sight appear insecure and dangerous, the natives often make trips to different ports of the island over a sea usually rough, and at a rate of speed almost phenomenal.

The picturesque and highly interesting Cingalese are a small and delicate race, exhibiting all the different shades of brown in their complexion and frequently verging upon a hue as black and shiny as may be seen in other races.

A heavy suit of black, lustrous hair, well oiled, and worn with a tortoise-shell comb, stuck through a neat coil at the back of the head, gives a distinctly feminine appearance, and at the same time intensifies the deep, serious expression of the eye, as well as the chiseled fineness of their cameo-like features.

A sort of skirt of white cotton, suspended from a girdle about the loins, reaches a little below the knee and aids in great measure the unmasculine appearance of the wearer. A goodly number, embracing those who toil in the more humble walks of life, wear only a kind of swimming tights, and a head covering of bamboo, especially designed as a protection against the rays of a tropical sun.

The home life of these simple people is, in most respects, without the slightest recognition of the claims of modesty or ordinary privacy; adjustable doors and windows, formed of a matting made from the fibre of the palm tree, are used only when a storm of wind or rain renders them necessary. The apparent looseness of custom, as regards their private affairs, does not seem to be the promoter of neighborly strife, as one might suppose; but, on the contrary, matters of untold importance seem to animate the brain and weight the bare, brown shoulders of young and old alike, leaving them but little time to look after the affairs of others; in this respect that development of our new world civilization known as the Grundys, "retailers and remodelers of news of all description," have placed before them a most worthy example.

Each of the little native huts has something of a garden about it, and in these, many of which are adorned and shaded by the luxuriant palm and the large fringed leaves of the graceful banana, much time is spent carefully tending their growing produce or hugging the shade in idle comfort.

I shall not attempt to tell the reader of the inexhaustible resources of this fruitful island, and will only say before pushing on to more personal experiences, that a wealth of rich mineral deposit of iron ore, lead, tin, and manganese, but slightly worked, affords opportunity for the successful development of the most fruitful mining operations.

Over four hundred of rare and valuable woods, including satin wood and ebony, contribute largely to the substantial prosperity of the island. The many different specimens of the palm, every part of which is adapted to the needs of man, is here luxuriantly prominent and is the most striking and pleasing feature in this paradise of tropical beauty. Salt, which is found in beds, is maintained as a monopoly by the government and is the source of a considerable revenue. Bread-fruit, coffee, tea, and cinnamon flourish abundantly, while rice, cotton, tobacco, and pepper, are extensively grown.

The many rare and beautiful varieties of plants met with on every hand and at every step of the stranger's progress calls forth the most genuine admiration, and to the naturalist, volume upon volume of choicest information are here spread before him.

CHAPTER IX.

CEYLON AND THE CINGALESE.

UPON invitation of Mr. Matthews, one of the wealthiest merchants of the island, and from whom the supplies of coal and provisions for our ship were purchased, C—— and I spent several hours very pleasantly at his place of business during our first visit ashore, and to his kindly courtesy, and that of his confidential clerk, Mr. Stewart, we were indebted for many attentions, which, in great measure, made our stay at Colombo a pleasant memory.

Our host was a native of Ceylon, of large stature, just in the prime of life, his smooth rich skin was somewhat darker than the average, while every feature of an almost perfect face told of the rare good nature for which he was justly famous.

His fine black hair was brushed smoothly back from a high forehead and had the usual knot at the back secured by a comb of tortoise shell somewhat larger than those commonly used. A double-breasted white duck coat, fastened all the way to his chin with shining naval buttons, gave a semi-official tone to his stalwart form.

The native skirt or habit of white material girdled beneath the coat reached nearly to his feet, the soles of which were protected by sandals made from the fibre of the palm.

When going from place to place looking after his varied interests, Mr. Matthews usually carried a huge sun-shade of bamboo silk in lieu of other head covering, and I have more than once been impelled to turn and look with admiration upon the calm dignity of his noble figure.

On this occasion he gave us in charge of his clerk, who invited us to "tiffin" in his bachelor apartments located on the upper floor of the building. Mr. Stewart was a thoroughly "up-to-date" young man of Indian and English extraction. Nature had dealt most generously with him, as concerns both form and feature, and several years of travel spent in the social and artistic centers of Europe had developed in him a culture and refinement seldom met even in the polite circles of the Orient. He was about thirty years of age, of lively disposition, and, in an entertaining manner, recounted to us many of his experiences in other lands. He had intended while abroad spending six months traveling in the United States, but was forced to abandon his desire and return to England at the end of the first month, on account of, as he forcibly expressed it, the abominable prejudice shown by Americans against persons of dark skin. He said, on arriving at New York, and after a tedious wait upon the Custom's officials, he was driven to one of the leading up-town hotels. Presenting himself at the office, an insolent clerk, who, if it were not for his unbounded arrogance, might have been mistaken for the owner, met his inquiry for a room, by the statement that they were "full." At this time his uneasy glance observed the foreign marks upon a valise the porter had rested on the counter, and, in a somewhat pleasanter tone inquired, "Where are you from?" The answer seemed satisfactory, for he was permitted to register and made a stay of several days, a most conspicuous, though not wholly welcome guest.

He said that he met a great many people of color in Boston and Washington, who were fitted, intellectually and socially, to adorn any sphere, and he could not understand why this system of caste should operate to the detriment of such a worthy and self-respecting class of citizens, and, at the same time, allow the low, vicious, and ignorant overflow from foreign countries to find toleration, if not a cordial welcome.

Our "tiffin" was a most pleasant little affair served by a well-trained native boy (all male servants are "boys" in the East. This one was at least forty-five), in a large airy room, having numerous openings or windows reaching from roof to floor, and offering a cordial welcome to every breeze. The rays of the sun were excluded by means of the low overhanging eaves of the roof, a feature common to the architecture of the Indian countries.

We might have been disposed to linger in these pleasant surroundings some little while after the meal had ended, but we found to our surprise it was past three o'clock, and, not knowing how long our ship would remain in port, we were constrained to put to good use every moment of time in order that we might lose as little as possible of the novel beauties of this interesting island.

At the suggestion of Mr. Stewart, a carriage was called, and a delightful drive filled in the remaining hours of the afternoon. We started about the time the native population begins to recover somewhat from the depressing effects of a midday tropical sun, and about each little hut along the route there was seen a family group, the elders engaged about house or garden, while the scantily clad youngsters sported gleefully in the shade of banana or palm tree. In a very short while we had arrived at the Museum of Ceylon, situated a little beyond the city on one of the beautiful roads traversing the Cinnamon Gardens, and spent an hour under the instructive guidance of our friend, in looking over its rare collection of rich and curious treasures.

A well-selected library containing many rare and valuable works occupied a large space of the first floor, while the remaining portion was given to the display of ancient inscriptions, representations of antiquated human and animal species and sculptured images of deities worshiped in past years, many of which were hideously unnatural and repulsive.

The central figure in this unusual group was a mammoth specimen of the elephant of India splendidly mounted and appearing so natural that one might easily imagine him making a pathway through the thickets of his native forests.

In another department was an exhaustive display of the fish peculiar to the waters of that section, ranging in size from the tiniest of finny creatures to that of the mighty whale, the whitened bones of whose Leviathan frame impressively suggested the wonderful strength of this monster of the deep. On the second floor was seen much to excite the interest of the casual observer, and the student of natural history might spend with great advantage several days looking through so valuable a collection of native exhibits. The main hall of this floor was given to a display of animals such as the tiger, wildcat, wild boar, porcupine, bear, and different specimens of the monkey tribe. Some of these had begun to show the wear of time, principally, as Mr. Stewart informed us, from a lack of proper attention. In another smaller room, large glass cases were arranged along the wall showing many varieties of insects, some of which were particularly noticeable for the exquisite beauty and delicacy of their tints, developing in several instances the most unusual effects in light and color. In other cases placed in the center of the room, and around which a protecting railing had been built, were displayed a wealth of glittering gems, while on a cushion of purple velvet in a separate case were shown the jewels worn by the ancient rulers.

Another interesting exhibit was found in the collection of curious coins, being specimens of the different forms of money used from a remote period to the present time; these varied in size from the head of a tack to that of a silver dollar, all bearing a peculiar device, the most common of which was a tree or flower or some native animal.

By far the most elaborate as well as instructive of

the several departments of the Museum was the display of the many products derived from the cocoa-nut palm, a few of which were oil, wine, food, sails, nets, rope, matting, pans, plates, cups, torches, and an array of other articles considered indispensable in the daily life of the Cingalese.

It was nearly sunset, and the keeper was closing the building for the night, when we at last stood without the shadow of the great arched doorway. The driver was sweetly dreaming of what he should charge us for the season of comfortable idleness he was enjoying, while his shadowy steed sought to round out his ancient anatomy by browsing along the green turf of the well-kept lawn.

Mr. Stewart suggested that the evening was the best time to witness something of the rites of Buddhism, and as there was no necessity for an early return aboard ship, the driver was ordered to take us to the Temple of Buddha.

The road over which we now made our way was an ideal picture of tropical beauty and luxuriance.

An unwonted calm seemed to have settled over all nature. The mellowed rays of the fast declining sun fell in lengthened shadows of gold and crimson over broad-leaved palm and fruited cocoa, and threw a halo of fading brightness far and near, o'er hut and grove. We were made aware of a nearer approach to the temple by a hideous confusion of sounds from various instruments, mingled in hearty discord. Coming within view we noticed a throng of natives passing in and out of the gateway to the sacred enclosure; those entering carried a bunch or small basket of

INTERIOR OF BUDDHIST TEMPLE.

beautiful flowers, designed, as we soon learned, for an offering to be placed on the altar of their devotion.

Our presence created much comment, and for a time the disciples of Buddha wavered in their mission of duty and reverence, and observed our party so closely, that, had it not been for the companionship of our friend, I confess I might have felt a little uneasy. In our turn, we passed within the enclosure, and were face to face with the musicians who had entertained us at a distance. There were five of these, partially resembling in their make-up and actions the burnt cork favorites of the modern footlights.

These instruments were two tom-toms, an odd looking sort of drum giving forth a flat and unearthly sound, and a pair of flutes. We stood for some time watching these performers, whose functions seemed akin to the trick resorted to by the management of low-priced theatres in large cities, who have the band play in front of the house before a performance to attract the rabble. Arches of evergreen leading diagonally to the two doors of the building gave a festival appearance to the enclosure, which was otherwise decorated with a profusion of wreaths and flowers. The building itself was of circular shape, having a cupola in the center of its projecting roof of red tiling. The one large room was divided by a full-length partition traversing its center, on either side of which were paintings setting forth the different characteristics of Buddhism. Opposite the door by which we entered and on a platform which extended around the the room was a mammoth figure in wax representing the present Buddha; the limbs were moulded in perfect symmetry, the hand small and tapering, the cheek a delicate vermilion, and, apart from its divinity, in which the native firmly believes, challenged more than a passing notice as purely an evidence of artistic skill. There was depicted on an extensive screen in the rear of the building an elaborately executed painting delineating the history of Buddhism, showing the difficulties encountered in finding an eligible divinity, selecting at first all sorts of animals, which were derided and rejected by the Devil, until at last, after much speculating and indecision, a female was presented, accepted, and confirmed by his Satanic Majesty. The adherents of this faith are now, however, possessing their souls in patience while waiting for the coming Buddha, who is expected during the next thousand years. The guide, who explained the various emblems and rites of worship, was an official of the temple, and treated us to an interesting discourse concerning this strange scheme of religion; he failed to enlighten us, however, as to whether or not the choice of a female for the divinity was due to any consideration on his majesty's part, that he might use her to better purpose in his many subtle schemes for dominion and conquest.

Another form of worship next claimed our attention, the high priests of which were several lesser divinities, each occupying a section of the platform.

The figures were formed of alabaster, heroically proportioned and of beautiful mould. To these, the control of one especial subject or element, such as the crops, fire and water, love and maternity, etc., is given, and on the altar of these the natives placed beautiful flowers and besought their mediation to secure a desired blessing. There comes to everyone, perhaps, who is brought within the influence of strange religions, a feeling of solemn wonder and skepticism; we look down from the heights of what we consider a superior consciousness, and are apt to say, with the lordly Pharisee, "I thank God I am not as other men;" "*I am better than thou;*" but to my mind there was something pathetic about the absolute devotion of these simple people; an evidence of rock-ribbed faith and utter dependence, that is seldom equaled by the devotees of other creeds.

After all, the consolations of religion cannot be confined within the boundaries of any one particular faith, and the simple formula, "*I take refuge in Buddha,*" which is each day repeated by more than four hundred millions of human beings, invite, at least, the respect of the Christian world, even as it has proved their inspiration and comfort since many years before the Christian era.

The season of twilight, so full of magic charm and beauty in other latitudes, is of brief duration in the tropics; so short, indeed, is it as to appear an almost immediate transition from daylight to darkness.

It was about seven o'clock when, emerging from among the Buddhist emblems, symbols, images, and other insignia of the temple, we found the sable draperies of night had already fallen about nature's footstool, while the light of the stars, brilliantly luminous in the clear vault above, developed bogy shadows, great and small, among trees and huts the region round.

We learned through the guide who had so courteously instructed us in the mysteries of Buddhism, that the day was an anniversary and celebrated as a religious holiday and festival; we were not surprised, therefore, to encounter, a little later, a straggling procession of several hundred half-clad natives bearing each a flaming torch or some other means of illumination.

Several musicians of the kind previously noticed at the temple headed the column, and immediately in the rear of these, on a wooden form covered with flowers, was borne by two natives an image of the Buddha. We dismissed the carriage shortly after leaving the temple and made our way single file along the route of the procession.

The huts were unusually brilliant with many tapers, and just in front of each had been built a stand, upon which, confusedly piled, appeared a variety of the most fragrant flowers.

An incident which furnished us much amusement and in which the laugh was at the author's expense, occurred towards the close of the evening : while passing a hut where the floral display seemed unusually attractive the thought came to me that I might appropriate a single bud and, by pressing, keep it always as a souvenir of this Buddhist celebration; accordingly, I had reached forward with outstretched hand, when a small stick fell across my knuckles with a resounding "whack." I had reckoned without counting the very old and decrepit native woman who, seated within an angle of the door, watched with jealous care lest the beauteous buds and blossoms, betokening her abiding trust in the Buddha, should be despoiled ere the procession passed. Our first day's acquaintance with Ceylon and the Cingalese was rounded out with an eight o'clock dinner at the Queen's Hotel. Here, as in centers more given to fashion, dinner is the event of the day, and for this meal society wears her brightest smile and daintiest toilet. Mr. Stewart accompanied us afterwards to the quay and saw us safely off for the ship, which, by the aid of a briskly-sailing outrigger, we soon reached, and were in the shortest possible time repeating in the land of dreams the varied experiences of the day.

On Thursday, August 3d, liberty was granted aboard ship, and after quarters and inspection at nine o'clock the port watch, dressed in clean white uniforms and white cap covers, was sent ashore for twenty-four hours.

The Captain did not dine aboard that day, and our duties being ended with the one o'clock luncheon, C—— went ashore shortly after on business, engaging to meet me on the "Cricket" grounds at 5.30, where, from four o'clock until nearly dark, is witnessed a most animated scene; the athletically inclined of the foreign population, together with the younger members of the upper class native families, have here a favorite resort for sport and recreation, while on stated occasions large crowds are drawn thither to witness the match games of cricket or lawn tennis between the several teams.

J

I found C—— at the appointed time playing at "catching ball," in true American style, with several Englishmen; and after exercising with them about an hour we left the grounds in company with one who was introduced as Mr. Clarkson.

At his suggestion we strolled over to "Galle Face" and took a "turn" among the Cingalese beaux and belles. Mr. Clarkson was a conductor on the English railway, with headquarters at Colombo, and had come out in that capacity in 1875; at the end of three years he had become so enamored of the country, and a certain native lady whom he made his wife, as to conclude to make Colombo his home. We left the "promenade," and, being loth to part with so congenial a companion, prevailed on Mr. C—— to accompany us in a drive.

We found upon our return that we were too late for dinner at the Hotel, and so concluded to take a lunch at the Café. The public house to which we resorted was a rambling one-storied affair, comprising bar, dining, billiard-room, and kitchen, the first three opening directly the one into the other, and separated by a slight wooden partition about four feet high. Our lunch consisted of a very excellent variety of fish, nicely cooked, and an enjoyable "curry" of chicken, which caused a sort of pins-and-needles sensation to linger on our palates several hours thereafter, and which the several brands of liquid refreshments resorted to were powerless to remove. It was nearly eleven o'clock when, after playing several games of billiards, we were passing out through the bar-room, there was heard a noise of scuffling and of several angry voices, and immediately there rushed in two of the sailors from the *Ossipee*, both in a state of semi-nudity, their clothing having been lost in the brawl, while what remained was torn and gashed in many places. One of them was bleeding profusely from a wound in the forehead and both were in a state of extreme intoxication. The proprietor came from behind the bar to try and right matters, and was furiously attacked by Mc—— a petty officer aboard ship, who, swinging a chair in one hand and lunging at him desperately with a knife in the other, ran him into the street. We saw there was no good end to be gained by mediation or by attempting to stem the current of rage in the liquor-maddened brutes, so, after a whispered consultation, our party disappeared through a window and watched the progress of events from the veranda. Mc—— and his companion reappeared after a few moments, and, after the style of the old time "Bowery" thugs, proceeded to do everything in sight. A western cyclone or destructive blizzard could have scarcely have left more wreckage in their trail than did these two Americanized sons of old Erin. Everything "went," the mirror was shattered out of all recognition, glass after glass was hurled with vengeful force among decanters and bottles, the contents of which ran wild over the floor in a stream of drunken riotousness; chairs and tables were knocked off their pins and left without a leg to go upon. By this time a throng of natives had gathered outside and were in a pitiful state of fear and excitement caused by the violence of these barbarous westerners. When at last they left the building, finding nothing more to destroy, they dashed out among the crowd, the echoes were awakened far and near by the shrieks of women, men, and children who fled in all directions, their garments of white producing a series of nimble-footed silhouettes as they disappeared among the neighboring trees. The affair was brought to the notice of the Captain next day by the much-injured proprietor and adjusted by the payment of damages out of the pay account of the offending sailors. They were also further punished by ten days' solitary confinement, a six-months quarantine, and in addition the petty officer suffered humiliation by the loss of his official "Yellow Jacket."

On Saturday, the 9th, I left the ship in company with Mike, the steerage steward, having agreed to make an excursion to the exile home of Arabi Pasha, ex-Khedive of Egypt. C—— was unavoidably detained aboard ship, and was also compelled to forego the dinner given in our honor by Mr. and Mrs. Clarkson.

A drive of a little less than two hours over a road giving evidence of neglect, strangely contrasting with others so perfectly kept, and leading through a part of the island luxuriously wild with towering palms, giant creepers, and knotted trees of most curious shape, brought us to the gates of the ex-Khedive's retreat. These, paint-worn and dilapidated, were flung wide in cordial welcome, and our approach to the house was through a partially shaded avenue, sadly overgrown with weeds and showing but faintly any trace of wheels. On every hand were evidences of lack of attention and cultivation. Plants, trees, and vines had been allowed to run together in the most prodigal disorder.

A low, wooden structure, plain and simple, built on the highest part of the grounds, affords a shelter to the man who a short while ago might choose his residence from among a dozen famous palaces.

We alighted in front of the main entrance and gave a few strokes with the rusty brass knocker on the half-open door, which sounded out clear and distinct in the ominous quiet which enwrapped the place. No sign of life save that inferred from an array of easy chairs and ottomans about the veranda was visible, and we had nearly lost hope of an answer to our summons when we were startled by a girlish peal of merry laughter followed by the slow approach of slippered feet. We were, of course, thinking only of his excellency, and concluded that these slippered feet were an important part of the anatomy of that once august personage.

We were, therefore, surprised and disappointed when there appeared in the doorway a young man about the age of twenty-five, tall and slightly made; his otherwise pale and expressionless face was redeemed by a pair of fine black eyes, which beamed upon us pleasantly and inquiringly for a moment before extending his hand in cordial greeting. We craved indulgence for the intrusion, and said that we felt unwilling to leave the beautiful island of Ceylon without affording ourselves the honor of a visit to the present home of the ex-Khedive. He replied that his father was always pleased to see Americans, for whom he cherished the fondest regard, and regretted that the accustomed daily siesta which his parent was now enjoying should preclude the possibility of his meeting us.

It was now nearly four o'clock, and, after a cordial hand-shake, we resumed our carriage and hastened back to town. "Mike" went immediately aboard the ship, while I repaired to the hotel to keep my appointment with Mr. Clarkson. Punctually at six he arrived, having driven direct from the station, which he had just reached on his return trip from Candy. After brushing up a little and partaking of some slight refreshments, we set out for his home.

A pleasant drive of an hour brought us to a beautiful, vine-clad cottage, the central portion of which was octagon-shaped, having a wing at either side, with the usual veranda traversing the front; the appearance of this, with its inviting hammocks, comfortable chairs, and children's toys, bespoke its constant use in the daily life of the family. Here I was presented to Mrs. Clarkson, who, with her two beautiful children, a girl and boy of six and four, respectively, had come to meet the husband and father.

The home was an ideal one, furnished simply, though tastefully, with the products of native skill and industry.

Nothing foreign was to be seen except a few portraits adorning the wall, among which were those of the mother and father of the host, and a splendid grand piano occupying a corner of the cozy little parlor.

Mrs. Clarkson possessed a beauty of face and form rarely seen among the Cingalese, being tall and exquisitely moulded in every detail of her well-rounded figure, and supported her matronly dignity with an engaging frankness and charm of manner that would make her a favorite in any circle of culture and refinement.

The dinner was entirely *en famille*, the children's "early-to-bed" custom being suspended on this occasion; and I was given also the additional pleasure of meeting a sister of the hostess, a young lady of seventeen, as yet in school, whose active and inquiring mind afforded smooth and ready change to a remarkable variety of subjects, and infused an agreeable vein of spiciness through the general conversation. A cup of excellent coffee and an accompanying cigar, in which Mr. C—— and I indulged after the withdrawal of the ladies, had their sequence in various interesting reminiscences recounted by the host of his life among the Cingalese. The remainder of the evening was filled in with music by the ladies, during which several native pieces were sung and interpreted, delighting the ear by a singularly pretty melody, and showing a wealth of tender sentiment in their sweetly simple composition. A generous assortment of curious and interesting bric-a-brac was duly exhibited and admired, as well as a large album of family and other native pictures, from which I was permitted by madam to take an excellent likeness of her husband.

The evening so delightfully spent in this happy home passed all too swiftly, and when, towards eleven o'clock, I essayed to take my leave, it was only to receive an emphatic veto, and I was persuaded to accept further hospitality for the night.

Before retiring I enjoyed a cigar in the garden with Mr. C——; all nature seemed hushed in a perfect calm, while myriads of stars, those lustrous children of night, had seemingly pooled their brilliancy in rivalry of their absent queen. Musing on this tranquil scene, I thought of Byron's line, "At night an atheist half believes in God"; and I felt, indeed, that the enlightened soul, living amidst these countless evidences of God's handiwork and denying His existence, was infinitely worse than the poor Indian, "who sees God in clouds and hears Him in the winds." When leaving next morning the madam presented me with a package of native nuts and an exquisitely carved sandal-wood box, containing a variety of odd and beautiful shells, which she hoped would often lead me to think, when again I should be in America, of my friends in their far-away island home.

Mr. Clarkson drove in town, and before going aboard ship I took an early morning stroll through the quaint little bazaar or market-place. The general stock consisted of a variety of fresh and delicious fruits exposed for sale on the broad leaves of the banana.

Here one may see piles of cocoanuts, great bunches of bananas, immense bread fruit (seemingly bursting with meaty ripeness), sweet-smelling pineapples, and vast quantities of juicy mangoes and custard fruit.

Somewhat removed and in a group by themselves are found the fish-dealers, whose wares, both fresh and dried, make a direct and not altogether savory appeal to the unaccustomed nostril of the stranger. The ingredients for the favorite Indian dish of "curry" may also be purchased here. The variety of this article of food most generally used among the natives is made of rice, simply boiled, with a sauce whose chief substance is some kind of fish or animal meat, highly seasoned with pepper or leaves possessing a peculiar aromatic flavor. There is utilized for this purpose nearly every variety of fish or animal, and by skillful seasoning many delightful surprises to the palate are furnished.

August 14th. At last, after several days of unclouded pleasure, we are leaving this land of infinite natural delights. We shall, perhaps, never visit its peaceful shores again, but the future cannot hold too much of either joy or sorrow but what additional pleasure or consolation will be found in recalling its bright skies and gorgeous sunsets, the rare and beautiful varieties of its flora, the peculiar charm of its spice-scented atmosphere, and the childlike simplicity of its dark-skinned people, which places them on a plane of ideality among the races, and wins for them the friendly consideration of the civilized world.

CHAPTER X.

LIFE AMONG THE CHINESE.

"LAND HO!" shouted by the lookout early on the morning of the 22d, tells us that we are again drawing near to a strange and still more distant shore. The traveler, however, will become exceedingly weary if he keep a continuous watch from the time he first hears this cry until his feet are permitted to tread the soil of Singapore. Numerous islands of various shapes and sizes, richly clad with verdure and abounding with all kinds of tropical animal life, greet the eye on all sides and make of the passage through the Straits of Malacca an ever-changing panorama of natural beauty and grandeur. There is also considerable danger attending the trip on account of the many windings and abrupt turns of the channel, which in some places is very narrow, and, in consequence, a continued and steady vigilance is maintained on chart and compass by those in command. The captain and navigator of the *Ossipee* exercised the utmost care from the time land was sighted, and to them, at least, came a most welcome relief when, at three o'clock on the afternoon of the 23d, we were safely moored to the dock at Singapore.

Knowing that the length of our stay here depended

entirely upon the facility with which the vessel could be coaled, and naturally curious to see something of the strange people at the different ports visited, I obtained the captain's consent for a brief run ashore the day after our arrival.

Singapore, with the other province of the straits settlements, Malacca and Wellesley, and the numerous islands lying off the extremity of the Malay peninsula, came into the possession of the English in 1824.

They were then but sparsely inhabited, save by a few barbarous tribes and wild animals, and the price paid was $60,000 and a life annuity of $24,000 to the Sultan of Jehore, by whom they were deeded in fee simple. The subsequent commercial history of the settlement has eminently vindicated the wisdom of the transaction on the part of old England, and to-day, under her careful and energetic control, a considerable revenue is derived from many enterprises and the thorough development of rich natural resources.

Situated at the head of the Straits of Malacca, which lead directly into the South China Sea, Singapore commands the trade of Southern Asia and the islands of the Eastern seas, while its splendid facilities for the fitting out and repair of vessels of the largest size confirms its importance as a convenient resort for the ships of every nation. My time here was too short to afford more than a cursory view, and was spent chiefly in the west side, which contains the great mercantile ware- and counting-houses, and in a short drive among the neighboring hills, upon which are situated the country houses of many foreign residents. The population, estimated in 1883 at 200,000, consists of Chinese, Malays, Europeans, Eurasians, and other natives from the islands round about.

These are all quartered in different sections, and each shows by contrast a marked individuality, distinctly noticeable even on the shortest possible acquaintance.

As may be imagined, everyone was anxious to hasten on to China, and it was with great pleasure I learned, on returning aboard at sunset, that the ship would be coaled on the morrow, and we would leave early the day after for Hong Kong.

To C—— and myself the leaving of Singapore on the morning of the 25th was of more than ordinary import, as we had concluded to ask for our discharges either there or at Shanghai and try life among the Chinese for awhile, at least.

This idea was not the result of any dissatisfaction, but the outgrowth of a spirit of adventure, strengthened by the belief that we might secure more remunerative employment and be able to save a snug sum before returning to America.

All our leisure moments while sailing up the China Sea were given to the discussion of prospects and ways and means, and through repeated consultations with Joseph Ah Fah, the Chinese ward-room cook, whose home was Hong Kong, we concluded that the $150 to our credit on the paymaster's books would see us through until work was procured. "The best laid plans of men and mice oft gang a gley," however, and we shall see how these developed. It was confidently expected, in view of the season of the year, that we would encounter a storm on this trip, but aside from a heavy fall of rain at intervals during the first day the passage was for the most part pleasant. Excellent use was made of the good weather, looking to the perfecting of the ship's company in the various drills and manœuvres in order that a creditable showing might be made to the Admiral on the occasion of his official inspection, to take place shortly after our arrival on the station. On Saturday the 30th, we were speeding along with sail and steam at the rate of twelve knots and we expected to make Victoria Bay, Hong Kong, early Sunday afternoon, but approaching bad weather being indicated by a falling barometer Saturday night, led to the usual precautions of a reduction of sail, and consequent slackening of speed, which was still further decreased when towards morning we ran into a thick fog. Our progress was necessarily very slow, and we were much gratified when late in the afternoon the atmosphere began to clear, and again forging ahead at full speed reached an anchorage about ten o'clock Sunday night.

Every sign of the mist of the preceding day had disappeared, when, at five o'clock on the morning of September 1st, I came on deck and had a first view of the harbor and city of Hong Kong. Hundreds of crafts, both native and foreign, rested at anchor on the bosom of the quiet water. Two English war vessels and a French gunboat lay well in towards the shore and appeared like grim sentinels, strangely contrasting with an otherwise peaceful scene.

Looking shoreward, the eye encounters a range of

irregular and barren hills extending in circular form, and almost entirely sheltering the harbor on three sides, and affording a safe retreat from the dreaded typhoon which rages along the coast during a certain period of each year.

The bay is a magnificent sheet of water, covering an area of ten miles, and of sufficient depth to accommodate vessels of the largest size. On the top of the highest hill is the signal station, which by gun and flag flashes the news of vessels arriving and departing, and at the base of this, reaching well up the side, terrace above terrace, is built the greater portion of the city, which stretches out on either side along the water front. A sea wall of solid masonry extends around the harbor, and is a safeguard against the storms which now and then make their influence felt even within the unusually placid bay.

About six o'clock the little creeks which flow between the hills, affording a shelter to numerous small craft, turned loose upon the harbor a stream of these nightly tenants, and in a short while the port side of our ship was alive with a swarm of moon-featured celestials waiting to come aboard at the breakfast hour to solicit the laundry work of officers and men. Tailors, compradores (dealers in ship supplies), shoemakers, jewelers, artists, hatters, curio-dealers, and tradesmen of all kind seem to have been apprised of our arrival, and were on hand showing testimonials from the officers of American vessels formerly on the station, and with their usual persistence, flattery, and obsequious humility did they lay their plans for the gathering in of many American dollars. Our sailors are considered splendid game among foreign tradesmen, and are therefore welcome visitors in every port. Their wages are better and allowances more liberal, and with their impulse when ashore to paint everything they see or touch in colors of deepest crimson, it may be said that each town is virtually theirs for the season of their liberty. The boys of the *Ossipee* were no exception to this general rule, and when, at the end of the first week of our stay, liberty was granted, several branches of trade in particular received an unwonted impetus, while Jack had the satisfaction of spending "like a prince" in a few short hours the result of months of hardship and toil.

Hong Kong ranks first among the commercial marts of the East, and has grown since its cession to the English, in 1861, from a straggling village of 2,000 semi-barbarous fishermen to a splendid city of stone and brick, boasting a population of over 200,000.

The general population of China is greatly augmented by those who have no residence ashore, but who gain a livelihood by the aid of their little boats or sampans, as fishermen and acting as carriers for the many vessels frequenting the different sea-ports. The number of these quaint little water-abodes is estimated at 250,000, and allowing an average of four persons to each family (and there are often as many as eight), we have a grand total of 1,000,000 souls.

The English military are quartered on a height overlooking the harbor, and their mere presence, while strolling about the town clothed in her majesty's uniform, constitutes in itself a sufficient rebuke to any kind of native disorder.

The merchants are chiefly English and natives, while a number of East Indian firms have large establishments for the sale of beautiful silks, rich embroideries, etc. The stores of the natives along Queens Road are large and showy; and, ignoring pigtails and other concomitants of a Chinese character, one might easily imagine himself in one or another of the fashionable depots of America.

Queens Road is the principal thoroughfare, and during the day one sees a busy throng of natives and foreigners hurrying to and fro. The weather was very hot during our stay, and the inhabitants generally traveled armed with an umbrella or shade hat, the latter of cork or wide-brim straw.

The natives of the middle class were clothed in a cool, glazy stuff of one thickness, while the poor 'ricksha coolie, puffing, sweating, and trotting all day, divests himself of every article of clothing except his hat and a loin cloth of delicate proportions.

The evenings are usually pleasantly cool; the shops and streets take on a wonderful brilliancy from gas, electric lights, and a profusion of colored lanterns; the native theatres are in full blast; tea houses issue a fragrant invitation to the consumers of that delightful beverage; and each thoroughfare is alive with a teeming mass of rich and poor, high and low, seeking pleasure according to their various notions. The harbor, which may be viewed from several points along Queens Road, is an attractive sight, with its hundreds of lights, and the merry "halloa" of the sampan people, sculling here and there over the smooth surface of the water, may be distinctly heard.

On Sunday, the 7th of September, C—— and I spent the day ashore, and in the company of Joseph Ah Fah, the ex-wardroom cook, who had obtained his discharge, and was celebrating his reunion with Mrs. and a host of little Ah Fahs, spent several hours very pleasantly, and were enabled to see somewhat of the inner life of the Chinese. Through his recommendation, I left an order with Mr. Ah Nam, a native artist, for an oil painting of my mother. In connection with this, it has been my experience that a Chinaman of any craft whatsoever will never admit his inability to perform a piece of work. The painting in question was to be made from an old tin-type, very much faded, and I confess I believed it an impossibility to produce therefrom anything like a resemblance ; but, after studying it closely for awhile, he said, with a smile of confidence, "Yes! can do!" This painting now hangs in my home, and is considered by those who knew the subject a remarkably good likeness.

But one is apt to get the worst of most bargains with these folks, who are masters in the art of deceit and cunning; and however much John Chinaman may frown and wag his pigtail, and say, "Makee losee too much dollar, no can do," it is safe to say that when he posts his books the balance will be found on the proper side. Before going off to the ship that evening we stopped in a pawnbroker's establishment, where there was in progress an auction sale of unredeemed pledges. There were upwards of fifty natives in attendance, mostly men, who looked on with stolid indifference, while puffing their cheroots.

Each parcel as it was "knocked down" was handed over and tucked out of sight within the capacious clothing of the purchaser. There is something peculiarly fascinating about auctions; the more you stand and look the more you feel impelled to bid; and in this case, where the goods were unseen and consequently classed in your mind as *might be most anything*, I found the temptation irresistible; and in the seclusion of the pantry, a short while later, I, too, opened a little package, and beheld baby clothes wrapped around an ancient loaf of bread.

The colored American is in evidence here in China, and has contrived to secure a business foothold in several cities. Here at Hong Kong the Star Café was owned and operated by Mr. George Freeman, an old man-of-war's man, who had been discharged in 1875, and with his earnings laid the foundation of a prosperous business.

C—— and I were not sufficiently impressed with the outlook at Hong Kong; so concluded to delay applying for our discharges until we should arrive at Shanghai.

On Thursday, the 11th, a storm of great severity swept over the harbor, and during that day and night much damage was done to shipping and several sampans sunk, through which four Chinamen lost their lives, while the largest vessels, with every anchor dragging and steaming ahead to maintain their positions, were but little more than the playthings of the angry waters.

The Captain had accepted an invitation for that evening to dine with Colonel John S. Mosby, the celebrated guerrilla chief, whom President Grant appointed consul at Hong Kong. The storm rendered the keeping of the engagement impossible, and the dinner was deferred till the following Sunday.

Colonel Mosby held this position through several administrations, and has been for some time seeking reimbursement at the hands of the Congress in the sum of several thousands of dollars, which were collected during his consulship and turned over to the United States government.

On the 13th orders were received from Admiral John Lee Davis, commanding the Asiatic squadron, to proceed direct to Shanghai.

A pleasant passage of five days brought us to the mouth of the Yangtse-kiang, where we anchored about six o'clock on the evening of the 20th, and on the afternoon of the next day, Sunday, shifted to a position within half a mile of the city, and about four ships' lengths from the flagship, *Trenton*, and our sister ship, the *Juniata*, Captain Harrington commanding. A feeling of general satisfaction, which found expression in smiling faces and irrepressible good humor, inspired all hands, and, at sight of the proudly waving Stars and Stripes flying in gracious protection over hundreds of our countrymen here at the other side of the world, our hearts were filled with joy and pride for our grand and glorious America.

The band of the flagship played the airs which thrill the native breast, while, from the rigging of the two vessels, came a hearty welcome voiced in three rounds of lusty cheers. During the course of our stay abundant opportunity was afforded by exchange of visits aboard ship and through meeting ashore during the course of "liberty" for the forming and renewal of acquaintances among the fleet, and these meetings, to some of the older tars who had been together in former cruises, partook of the nature of a good old-fashioned Methodist love-feast, with "the flow of bowl" substituted for the "flow of soul."

The first four days in port were given to a thorough overhauling of the ship, the "hold" was "broken out" and restowed, which occupied the greater part of two days, and in every way the ship was put in condition for the inspection to take place on the 25th.

The ships of the fleet, now acting in concert in the matter of drill and naval manœuvres, were constantly on the *qui vive* in anticipation of orders signaled from the flagship, and each night and morning witnessed a spirited rivalry between the crews of the three vessels in a friendly race for first place as to the excellency and dispatch with which the orders were executed.

Inspection day dawned bright and clear. "All hands" were "turned to" at five o'clock, and by eight o'clock the ship presented an appearance thoroughly in keeping with the high standard main-

CAPT. JOHN F. McGLENSEY.

tained by the navy of Uncle Sam. At nine o'clock Admiral Davis arrived with his staff, and from half-past nine, when the crew was brought to muster, until three o'clock, with the exception of an hour for dinner, a most rigid inspection was held, embracing small-arm drill, "abandon ship," "fire quarters," and "clear ship for action." The admiral and party had luncheon in the cabin and left the ship at half-past three, after complimenting the captain upon the splendid showing made by officers and men.

The proposed action of C—— and myself, referred to in the last chapter, was settled to the satisfaction of all concerned in the following manner: The officers of most American war vessels doing service on the Asiatic Station are at great pains to secure as attendants either Japanese or Chinese, who, they claim, are more docile and industrious, and may certainly be fed at less cost than those of other nationalities. A monthly allowance of three dollars per head for their native diet will furnish the Chinaman a luxurious table and represents a saving of six dollars to the mess fund on the government ration of nine dollars per man. The relinquishing the service must, however, be voluntary on the part of those shipped in American waters; but the desired result is usually accomplished by one means or another, and during the remainder of the cruise, or as long as the ship is stationed in those waters, the creature comforts of our gentlemen tars are most assiduously catered to by the tidy little Jap or the solemn-visaged Chinese. The *Juniata* was expecting daily to be ordered home, and it was necessary that some immediate disposition be made of the Japanese and Chinese portion of her crew. To this end it was arranged for an exchange of the cabin attendants of the two vessels, and, as the proposition included our friend Louis, we agreed that the prospect of an early return to the states was to our best advantage; accordingly, on the 30th of September, at our request, C———, Louis, and I received our discharges from the *Ossipee* and a few hours later were reshipped aboard the *Juniata* for the remainder of her cruise.

Our duties were now in the main the same as formerly. We were, of course, surrounded by strange faces, but in routine work one vessel differs but little from another, and in a very short while we were as much at home as though no change had occurred. At the suggestion of Captain H———, who desired one of us within easy reach when he should be called on deck during the night in event of storm or any unusual circumstance, I stowed my mattress and blanket "aft," and each night made down a comfortable bed on the deck of the pantry. In the matter of "liberty," we found ourselves, if possible, even more favorably situated; the captain, who was known as "Black Jack" under the forecastle (presumably from his dark cast of countenance, which was emphasized by his heavy black beard and hair), while accounted one of the strictest disciplinarians in the service, was, withal, a pleasant gentleman of quiet manner and simple tastes. He told us to make ourselves at home in our own way, within the regulations, and added that he was anxious to get home like ourselves, and that he hoped to reach America early in the following spring.

Our friend William also bore a part in the general transfer, and was now duly installed as steerage steward of the *Juniata*, with the gratifying prospect of seeing his wife and little ones much sooner than he could have hoped.

Not knowing how soon the orders would arrive which would start us homeward, every available hour as well as dollar was *spent* ashore, absorbed in strange and curious sights and in the purchase of curios for remembrance gifts to friends and relatives and as souvenirs of the voyage.

The native city of Shanghai is enclosed by a high wall and moat, and is about three miles in circumference. It presents an aspect of filth and repulsiveness that can find no warrant even in the iron-bound conservatism of its people, and must forever be a loathsome picture in the memory of the temporary sojourner within its gates. The streets are small, and paved with large slabs of stone, long since obscured beneath a scum of dirt and mire.

It has its guild-halls and tea shops, and some of these are quaint specimens of Chinese architecture, while the Ching-hwang-main (city and moat temple) is built on an island of rock and is the most conspicuous from point of size and ornamental decoration.

There is little in the city that will agreeably entertain the visitor; so we turn from its uninviting prospect to a newer and more modern Shanghai.

The foreign suburb which chiefly constitutes

Shanghai, in the light of its later development, is divided into three parts, and embraces the English, American, and French concessions. The separation seems to be understood and recognized rather than known by any prominent line of division, and for all practical purposes may be regarded as one large city. The two principal buildings in the French concession are the cathedral and Hotel des Colonies, in the former of which I have spent several Sabbath mornings in attendance on divine service. On these occasions the entire body of the church was occupied by Chinese, while the rear seats were given up to several classes of younger folks chaperoned by their European instructors; the remainder of the congregation was made up of native half-castes, seamen of all nations, and a few European residents. Speaking generally, the foreign concessions contain many very handsome residences, with beautiful gardens, in which may be seen the skilled handiwork of the native culturist. Several large public buildings also adorn this quarter, noticeable among which are the Anglican Church and Masonic Temple, while the Shanghai Club, the most aristocratic organization of foreign residents in the Orient, is splendidly established in a handsome gray stone building facing the harbor on Yangtse Road. Many other houses of neat design are built along this broad and beautiful thoroughfare, which, with its numerous shade trees, general cleanliness, its bulwark of stone and stone jetties reaching here and there along its entire length out into the water, give to Shanghai one of the most beautiful river fronts in the world.

For the depth of about three blocks to the rear of Yangtse Road we find the large Hongs of native and foreign merchants. To the rear of these again are exclusively the smaller and more gaudy domestic shops. Traversing this section, one is impressed with the remarkable degree of sameness which apparently exists, and, taking a cursory glance, is apt to think a whole block utilized in one mammoth business. This is, however, due to the monotony of decorated signs, in which the dragon, variously painted or worked on silk, cotton, or paper of gaudy colors, is most conspicuous.

Foo Chow Road may be termed the "Vanity Fair" of Shanghai, and here one sees much of the fashionably dissolute life of the Chinese. During a stroll on a pleasant Sabbath afternoon my wandering steps took me in this direction. The day was, of course, in native esteem no more holy than another, but to Christian eyes the degree of license and prodigality was, at least, appalling.

Tea shops seemed to be doing a more than average business; sing-song houses were in full blast, and with gongs, bells, drums, and cymbals produced a resounding clatter of outrageous noises only equaled by some of the "musical features" of the "Midway" of our recent great Exposition.

The balconies of the various resorts were well patronized by females luxuriously lounging in silken robes, while sipping a favorite beverage or puffing away at a dainty cigarette. Vehicle after vehicle rattled along the roadway drawn by poor, unwilling steeds, each bearing a load of giddy butterflies or pompous pigtails, laughing, chatting, and given completely to the pleasure of the hour. Thinking since, calmly and dispassionately, I can but admit that this scene finds its counterpart on the Sabbath in some of our own large cities, and, allowing for the effects of local coloring, the reader need not go so far as Shanghai to see the reality of this picture. Passing through English town and on to the suburbs, in a short while China and all vestige of the Chinese is left behind. We first encounter a well-appointed race course, with beautiful stretch of lawn, commodious grand stand, and other necessary appurtenances; here the Shanghai Turf Club holds its meetings every spring and fall. Through the courtesy of the club, all man-of-war's men are complimented with free admissions.

The *Juniata* being in port during the spring meeting of 1885, a great many of the boys attended, and some, fortunate in picking the winners, found themselves well paid for their trouble. The exhibition was tame in comparison to the great events at Sheepshead Bay, Monmouth Park, and other noted resorts; yet every feature which added to the success of these were noticed, with various modifications, at the Shanghai course.

A goodly number of ladies were in attendance, and in their natty European toilets added grace and beauty to an unusually interesting scene. Chinese of all classes were strictly in evidence, and won or lost their bets with a nonchalance seldom attained save by the most accomplished sport. The Chinese Jocks rode admirably, and labored earnestly with both voice and whip to land a winner. There were a few accidents confined to the last event, the steeple chase, in which several riders were rather roughly used. Leaving the course, we enter upon a beautiful drive known as Bubbling Well Road; cottages of beautiful design, in the center of well-kept grounds, may be seen on either hand. Grand old trees, towering loftily and converging at the top, form an avenue of delightful shade, and judging from the many fine equipages to be seen any pleasant afternoon, the aristocratic element of this oriental city are duly appreciative of its rare charm and quiet natural beauty.

American-town comes last in point of location among the foreign concessions, and is very pleasantly and romantically situated at the extreme right of the harbor. The American consul has his establishment here, as also a few other American families.

The government machine shops and dry dock are located here, which contributes greatly to the business activity of the section. A good many natives also have their homes and shops within the concession, and are employed chiefly in the making of trunks and boxes of camphor wood.

Situated on Yangtse road, just at the bend of the stream which separates American from English town, is a beautiful little public garden. Its walks shady and scrupulously clean, flowers of variegated colors adorn its beds, while oriental plants and trees are arranged so as to form cool and inviting retreats. Thus, overlooking the river, it commands a view of the entire harbor, and is, all in all, one of the most delightful recreation grounds imaginable. There is a band employed by the city, which gives concerts every evening during the spring and summer, and this is the hearts' delight of hundreds of European young folks, and their Chinese nurses.

The port of Shanghai, from a business point of view, ranks among the foremost of China.

Near the Wusung Forts, there is a bar which, however, may be easily crossed by the largest vessels at high water. Opposite old Shanghai may always be seen hundreds of junks, ocean-going, and otherwise, lashed close together. Vessels of foreign nations are usually anchored opposite the foreign settlements.

The water course of the harbor of Shanghai is noted for the remarkable swiftness of its current; in this connection, I was one day during our first stay made an involuntary witness of a painfully sad and deplorable event; the hour was noon, and as is the case at each meal time, sampans innumerable lay along the side of the ship; the water was rougher than usual, and the little boats were tossing up and down to the rise and fall of every wave. When "turn to" sounded at one o'clock, there was a great rush of tailors, curio-dealers, and washer-men to leave the ship. One of the Chinamen, in stepping from boat to boat to gain his own, made a fatal miscalculation and was plunged headlong into the water; in the panic which ensued, one of the boats was overturned and the current bore it swiftly away. I happened to look out of the pantry port just as the poor Chinaman came to the surface, and saw him make one feeble effort to grasp a boat in passing; failing in this, he was borne rapidly away, and, rushing to the after-cabin port, I saw him throw up both arms above his head for an instant, and sink forever from sight. A cutter had been called away immediately at the cry of "man overboard," but after cruising around in the vicinity of his disappearance for more than an hour abandoned the fruitless search. The crew were successful in recovering the capsized boat, which was returned to its owner, who, at the time of the catastrophe, had saved himself by clambering over the side of another boat. This fatal accident was rendered doubly shocking by the fact that there were at least twenty Chinamen in their boats along the side, who, by putting out their hands as he passed, might have saved his life; instead, they looked on unfeelingly, and saw the terrible end with apparent composure.

Puzzling myself over this wanton indifference to so needless a sacrifice of human life, at the time, I have since learned, that the superstition of the people teaches them that a person in distress is the object of the anger of one or another of their gods, and to aid them in any way would not benefit the afflicted, but would in all likelihood transfer this anger to themselves.

In many ways did our intercourse with the Chinese demonstrate the truth of the saying "that they are a peculiar people," differing as they do in many points from western nations as to their physical, political, and social characteristics. They are indeed unlike any other people, but boasting a civilization antedating the Christian era by three thousand years, and bringing the same down to the present day, practically unchanged, their very conservatism challenges the admiration of the world, and bespeaks for them a place among the brotherhood of nations. In their physical features several types are presented, the extremes of which are, the high-born and the common people. Between these two classes, apart from the obliquity of their eyes there is little in common. The former, lords of the land, and glorying in the various signs which unerringly stamp their good birth, are looked up to with reverence and awe, the natural results of gross ignorance and superstition. The males of this class are generally of medium stature, and of a complexion varying between a yellow and a brown, according to the climate.

Their heads always well shaved, and queue oiled and neatly plaited, *a la mode*, together with an accompanying suit of rich flowing robes, make up the exterior of a gentleman as effectually as outward signs can and do in other countries. The Chinese lady embodies within her form and features the more palpable evidences of noble lineage. The natural whiteness of her skin, enhanced by the use of cosmetics; delicate penciled eyebrows; luxuriant wavy black hair done in the prevailing style and mounted with glittering ornaments; and her form enveloped in costly silks of various patterns, combine to place her beyond the pale of common mortals, while the crowning distinguishing mark, their little feet, gives them the prestige of a divinity.

On one occasion, there were two of these "little feet" visiting the ship in company of several Chinese gentlemen, and a few American missionaries.

The ladies had to be carried bodily over the gangway and supported at every step. They were, of course the objects of much respectful attention, and attracted to themselves much genuine sympathy. Their pedal extremities were the size of the corresponding dependencies of an ordinary doll, and encased in a little shoe that in its beauty would have set the average child mother wild with delight.

There were also many whispered conjectures as to whether or not with the contraction of the feet the limbs had grown proportionately larger, which question, in lieu of higher authority, science will perhaps take it upon herself to answer.

In contradistinction to these marks which are patent among the different classes of the nobility, there are those certainly which bespeak the individual of lower birth, of whom there are likewise several ranks; for instance, the proprietor of a "hong" will look with inconceivable disdain upon a simple workman, while the former, in his turn, is in great danger of taking a heavy cold when in the frigid atmosphere of a more extensive business man, and the poor "*coolie*," expecting nothing but the harshest treatment, is evidently thankful to be allowed the privilege of existing. As a rule the lower order may be distinguished in two ways, viz.: By a decided brown complexion and their dress, which, though conforming to the general style, is of common stuff and often selected with a view to economy rather than comfort.

Among the well-to-do, cleanliness is held in great esteem (cleanliness of dress), while with others nothing is more disregarded. I purposely make the distinction between cleanliness of apparel and that of diet, for as regards the latter the Chinese are firm supporters of the principle that "what will not kill will fatten," and are, accordingly, not so particular in their food and in the preparation of it for others as one could wish.

Their diet is chiefly rice, fish, animals (domestic and otherwise), and game, the last two having been carried through the process of "drying" so thoroughly as to leave its species a simple question of conjecture. Tea is the accustomed beverage, but in its preparation and use resembles, in name only, the substance in which Western nations take such delight. It is generally of the poorest kind, being obtained for as low as ten cents a pound, and used without sugar or other ingredient. But we must not at this stage linger longer with a subject about which volume after volume has been written without operating in the slightest degree to effect a diminution of the deep and universal interest concerning the land of flowers and its myriad inhabitants. We, therefore, invite our reader to go with us a little further along the Eastern seas and visit a neighboring people, dwellers of the land of the midnight sun and progressive subjects to the imperial throne of the Mikado.

CHAPTER XI.

JAPAN AND HER PEOPLE.

AT ten A. M. on the 14th of October the *Juniata* dropped anchor within the beautiful harbor of Nagasaki, and here, as at Hong Kong and Shanghai, we were immediately besieged by a swarm of small boats, each laden with the finished products or native skill to tempt the foreign purse.

The traveler rarely encounters scenery of more exquisite beauty than that which surrounds the quiet waters of Nagasaki Bay.

The city is picturesquely built within the shelter of numerous hills, richly clad with verdure, which, reaching out on either side in various shapes and heights, seemingly encircle the harbor, and from shipboard the impression is had of a splendid lake, whose peaceful bosom mirrors the reflection of floating clouds, romantic groves, temples on the hillside, and hundreds of curious craft of all sizes speeding here and there or at rest on the quiet surface.

The exact time of our start for home being as yet unknown, the crew generally felt they would be more than lucky if allowed to spend the interval amid such pleasant scenes. To further heighten the pleasure of our stay, the weather, which partook of the character of that season known as Indian summer for several weeks after our arrival, took on towards the latter part of November a crisp, frosty air, which rendered vigorous exercise a delightful recreation and conduced materially to the general health and good spirits of all on board. The men were treated most considerately as regards liberty, and, altogether, with the pleasing prospect of being early *en route*, it were difficult to imagine a more jolly and happy set. We found here the U. S. S. *Enterprise*, Captain Barker commanding, the Russian flagship *Warsaw*, an English cruiser, and two Japanese gunboats. The latter were splendid representatives of the new navy of Japan, trim and neat in every particular and thoroughly modern in every respect.

After a visit aboard the *Hokkaido*, during which a younger officer with true native courtesy escorted us through the different parts of the ship and in excellent English explained the various points of construction and mechanism, the impression remained with us that the Japs were not merely building a navy to decrease the treasury surplus nor wholly as a matter of national pride, but that when the occasion arrived it would be found that they had builded wisely and well in thus following the lead of the great powers in the matter of construction, equipment, and the many details of modern warfare.

The Japanese, however, are not essentially a people given to warfare, and the great success which has accrued to them in the recent tests of arms with their ancient neighbor, and which, to say the least, justifies the wholesale adoption of newer ideas and advanced methods, is not by any means their greatest glory. The simple arts and homely industries, in the perfection of which they stand without a peer, and which the acceptance of international polity, growing out of the Perry treaty of 1854 having brought within reach of the civilized world the marvelous products of native handicraft, clearly point to these as the royal road to national eminence. Any extended description of the Japanese, who have introduced themselves personally or by their wares to all countries and communities, is scarcely necessary in this brief narrative; the world has for many years seen him portrayed in more or less faithful representations upon imported articles, both useful and ornamental, and he is perhaps from this standpoint more truly cosmopolitan than other races. It is, however, through personal contact that one acquires an appreciation and regard for the many noble qualities of mind and heart which are met with among all classes and which appeal directly to the sympathy and friendship of the stranger. The extreme native courtesy met with on every hand without regard to rank is perhaps their most striking characteristic, and, indeed, to such an extent is this carried as to become a source of embarrassment to those of a more formal etiquette. Their business dealings are conducted in a manner at once liberal and open, and in pleasing contrast with the low cunning and deception so usual among eastern races.

Eminently hospitable, the country affords a welcome to the wanderer of every clan or clime, and the homely expression concerning the "latch string being on the outside of the door" never finds a more literal application than here. Jovial in their disposition and fond of sports and feasts and celebrations, they seem to possess the happy faculty of extracting pleasure from all sources, and on the slightest provocation a wrinkle of mirth will furrow the shaven head of the 'ricksha coolie or draw from between the ruby lips of the diminutive maid a merry ripple of innocent laughter. The average Japanese is of small physique though capable of wonderful endurance, and in the encounter of hardships develops a stoicism at once remarkable and admirable. The little fellows who are licensed as public carriers and are permitted a fee of ten cents an hour for one person, will pick up the shafts of their doll-like barouche and run off with you at the rate of six or seven miles an hour, and with an interval for a pull at their dainty pipes or to satisfy thirst at one of the many tea houses, will maintain such speed during the greater part of the day.

The native village presents an attractive study of the life and character of these interesting people: everything seems contrived on a scale of miniature proportions, from the ingeniously constructed and scrupulously neat wood and paper dwellings to the tiny brass bowls of their long-stemmed bamboo pipes. Frolicsome and light-hearted, yet withal industrious and toiling, they seem at all times to bring to their work, in whatever sphere, a cheerful and contented spirit, which is perhaps the best and truest help over the rough places along life's journey; so we find them patiently climbing, step after step, the lofty heights of material progress, the dead past of rock-bound conservatism and narrow prejudices left far behind, and before them the splendid achievements of their international sponsor, the Republic of America, as an incentive to still greater exertions.

The unblushing indecency and gross immorality until recently so generally practiced among the Japanese, and which found a strong and ready support in the brutish propensities of many depraved foreigners, is steadily giving way to an increasing sentiment in favor of virtue and morality.

To the enduring fame of the imperial throne, from whence this impulse springs, the standard of a higher and more noble womanhood is being continually elevated, and through the personal example and efforts of the empress, many important reforms have been instituted which have to a degree revolutionized the social system and advanced the kingdom many steps along the pathway of a nation's glory. The outrageous custom among females of blacking the teeth after marriage is gradually falling into disuse, and the native husband is beginning to appreciate with a western conception of the beautiful the original whiteness of nature's priceless pearls. The promiscuous use of licensed bath-houses which are commonly located within view of each passerby has been interdicted by the government, and the degrading and inhuman traffic by which the appetites of the lustful and vicious are catered to, and through which the appalling spectacle of a father placing an actual moneyed price on the immature charms of a youthful daughter, is gradually being retired before a higher moral tone and the disapproval of a modern civilization.

The population of Nagasaki is estimated at 150,000, with 2,000 Chinese who enjoy a monopoly of their home trade, and about 200 Europeans and Americans. The latter embrace the consular representatives, employes of various mercantile houses, and missionaries of the different denominations. The houses of foreign residents may be easily distinguished at a glance, being several times larger than the native dwelling and contrasting in many ways with the less pretentious habitations round about.

The little streets of the native city are wider than in Chinese cities, rigidly clean, and in a walk of an entire day one sees less that is repugnant to the senses than in an hour spent with their neighbors.

The principal road skirts the harbor, and along it are situated the Chinese and several of the foreign consulates. The Nagasaki Club, a commodious frame building of two stories, with its park and flower garden, is one of the principal features of the road. Among the chief industries of Nagasaki is the extensive carving and ornamenting of tortoise shell, and in this they exhibit wonderful skill. In the little shops of the dealers in this article one finds an assortment, both useful and ornamental, the finished product bearing an exquisite polish, and showing an almost marvelous delicacy of carving. Their work in bronze is also amongst the finest of the world, and through this they seemingly have sought to give an expression of their reverence for various honored customs of their love and worship of ancient heroes, and so a constant object-lesson of all that is considered worthy of emulation in the history of the race is afforded by what may be termed the highest class of national art.

Character painting upon china and other pottery has been wonderfully developed, and choice specimens of this work now find eager purchasers, and are accorded high rank both in private collections and national museums.

Paper is a native manufacture, and is made to serve a variety of uses, the most common of which are napkins and handkerchiefs, while in the peculiarly delicate construction of the native dwelling it is considered invaluable. The Japanese population is divided between the land and water, as with the Chinese. The little boats or sampans used by both countries are of the same general form and size, and in these they rear their families and attend to all matters pertaining to domestic economy. They are registered and licensed by the government as carriers, and are about twenty feet long by eight or ten broad. In the extreme rear or stern is the culinary department, which consists of a large pot very much in size and appearance like the *pot de feu* of a camping-out party. This is placed in a corner somewhat sunk between the bottom and the deck of movable boards, and in this they cook rice and other food. At mealtime the family collect in a squatting attitude around a circular tray containing the implements of war — chop-sticks and rice bowls — and falling to, wage a short but no less decisive battle. The little cabin for passengers in the center is constructed of bamboo hoops, forming an arch about four feet from the deck, and constituting the support of a sliding roof of bamboo matting, which is capable of so skillful an adjustment as to form an effectual watershed in case of rain, as well as a cool defense against the sun. On each bow is painted an eye, as is also the custom with the Chinese, by which device it is thought the boat is enabled to avoid the ordinary perils of the water. The manner of propelling is by sculling; there is a long, slightly elliptical, broad-bladed oar, working on a raised wooden pivot. The left foot is placed upon a narrow plane inclining towards the center, and with an easy and concentrated movement between hands and feet, often accompanied by a song of doubtful melody, the sculler sends his boat along with an incredible velocity.

The poorer class of Japanese, among whom the water people may be counted, seem inured to hardship, and go about during the coldest weather with bared legs and feet, the skin of which is often cracked and blue from exposure; to this they would pay no attention whatever, but seemed content so long as they were earning a few pennies. Their dress, at best, is very scant, consisting for male and female alike of a loose overgarment very much like a gentleman's dressing-gown, with the addition of large, flowing sleeves, the recesses of which are used as a repository for all sorts of small articles. The gown of the females is somewhat longer, and usually reaches to the ankle. A sash of broad, parti-colored material encircles the waist, and holds the habit together at that point, while the lower portion flows unconfined, and as they shuffle along in their wooden clogs much of the person is exposed to the gaze of the curious;

but this they do not seem to mind in the least. The sash is used only by the females as a support in carrying their infant burdens. At such time it is adjusted over the shoulders like a pair of suspenders, the child is placed inside the gown at the back, with one leg over each hip, and the sash drawn tight and tied in front.

I have often been amused at the sight of a child of seven or eight years, whose size would suggest the possibility of itself being carried, plodding along under the weight of its little brother or sister; with cheerful face, she (for they are always females so burdened) would shuffle on her way apparently unconcerned, the little one often asleep, its head lolling backwards and forwards; at other times, as though suffering no inconvenience, she would indulge with great zest in various childish games. The females, as a rule, take much care with their dress and general appearance. They are seldom homely, while the average are decidedly good looking.

Their hair is dressed in a style which is a more becoming and respectable edition of the butterfly fashion of the Chinese; by the use of a native oil, their rich wavy locks assume a glossiness but rarely equaled, — the figure enveloped in a dark habit of bright spots encircled by a gaudy sash, and the hair, with a single ornament, crowning a face from which beams a healthful freshness, form a picture peculiarly attractive to the stranger. Japanese custom does not permit the wearing of a pigtail by the men of the race, but it does insist that each manly pate shall be partly shaved, which makes many an otherwise comely person appear ridiculous, especially when, as is often the case, they are not well or regularly shaved; a kind of pants is worn, which are so closely fitted as to appear uncomfortable, and these seem to be the distinguishing features of the native dress. In the postal and customs service, and various other departments of the government, the employes are usually clad in a European costume, made of a black serviceable material. In every Japanese home, where garden space permits, may be seen the evidence of an innate love of the picturesque and beautiful; flower beds, arranged in many shapes and figures, bordered by rigidly clean foot-paths, bespeak a high order of native talent in this direction. A younger daughter of the house is the usual attendant of the little garden, and she may be often seen with water-pot in hand threading the tiny paths in the discharge of her self-imposed task.

In front of the smaller dwellings is often seen a skillfully adjusted and moss-grown rockery, having flowered plants protruding from between the crevices, and an artificial lake of one design or another lying placid at its base. On an afternoon in December, towards the end of our stay at Nagasaki, I left the ship about 5 o'clock, hoping to dispel a fit of gloominess that had hung about me all day, by a short run ashore. The weather was clear and cold, the wind, higher than usual, whistled drearily about the spars and rigging, and flecked the harbor with foam-capped waves which broke across the bows of the little sampans in frequent showers, and urged the patient sculler to his best exertions.

Hailing a shore boat I was soon sheltered within the little cabin in close companionship with the youthful members of the family, a pair of bright children, and what I at first thought a bundle of rags on the deck in a corner, but which soon developed a pair of promising lungs, and there was discovered to me a very curious morsel of humanity *a la* Japanese.

After landing, I went along the bund past the custom house, post and telegraph offices, and turned up the right bank of the first of many little creeks or inlets.

The water was now low, and scores of sampans, deprived of their necessary element, awaited the rising of the tide; some of the occupants busied themselves cleaning or repairing the boat, others puffed away at their little pipe, while another (I judge from their constant chatter), assuming an attitude more or less consistent with their ideas of comfort regaled themselves with the latest gossip. Children of both sexes and various sizes were ankle deep in mire in pursuit of tadpoles, minnows, and other such slippery things, to their evident enjoyment, and much to the detriment of their little fly-away gowns, and without the least regard for the chagrin of their parents or nurses.

After lingering here for a while much amused with the different sights, I turned the corner occupied by a tavern called the "City of Hamburg," kept by an exceedingly rickety person from the town of that name and his native wife, and was then in Japanese town. The street was filled with a succession of little shops, each with its stock artistically arranged for inspection. The entire front of these is made of bamboo and paper, easily adjustable, and are only put up at night and in case of storm. Passing the market, which consists of an assemblage of five or six stalls, I entered the great street of curios where may be found any quantity of specimens of exquisitely finished lacquer, crockery, tortoise shell, and silk embroidery, worked up in a variety of designs to suit the most curious fancy, as well as the deepest pocket. In the course of half an hour, I had left the most thickly-settled parts behind, and was traversing a section where shops were few and pedestrians scarce. The road was rough and broken, and I was often compelled to make detours in order to continue my way, passing now and again a native straggler who would eye me curiously, or a seedy looking "bonze" of one of the religious sects, of meek and lowly aspect, returning from the temple seen on the hillside. Ere long I was brought to a halt by a creek of greater dimensions than any previously seen. A heavy wall of gray stone, that must have been built years ago, ran along the bank on either side, and confined the stream which followed briskly its irregular course over a rocky bed. The sides of the wall, greenish, dry, and rusty looking, gave evidence that the water had at one time reached a much higher level; at intervals along its length were stone steps of uneven and crumbling appearance leading to the bottom, and now and then might be seen a diminutive barefoot maiden descending, bearing water scales to be filled from the stream below.

On the right wall stood an immense water-wheel, green and rotten with age, its huge skeleton frame having lived out its season of usefulness, and turning but slowly and indifferently with the force of the wind, had become a sort of "Ferris Wheel" for rest and observation to thousands of Japanese sparrows and their mates.

Directly opposite and at a distance of about fifty yards stood the symbol of the prevailing religion of the land, a Buddhist temple, its outer ornaments worn and faded by time and tempest, but, withal, an object venerated and loved by the native believers in the scheme of religion laid down by the great Indian teacher.

The shades of night were now fast descending; numerous gray slabs in the "silent city" adjoining the temple became all too spectral in the somber quiet, and urged a speedy return towards the brightly shining lights of the city and its peaceful harbor.

Pursuant to instructions from the admiral, our very pleasant stay at Nagasaki was ended December 4th, at 11 A. M., at which time we weighed anchor, and steamed away on our return to Shanghai, arriving there on the 7th. It was expected we would leave here almost immediately for Hong Kong, *en route* to the United States, and no more disappointed and disheartened crew ever manned a ship than that aboard the *Juniata*, when, after anxiously waiting until the 15th, orders were received which would keep us on the station at least four months longer. This material change in our prospects was in consequence of the French-Chinese war then in progress, and we were to proceed as early as practicable up the Min River, and remain during the unpleasantness in protection of American interests.

CHAPTER XII.
A WINTER IN CHINA.

IT was probably the wish of the entire crew of the *Juniata* that they be allowed to spend the approaching holiday season here, where a jolly good time might be expected more than at any other Oriental port. It would also seem from the fact that the boilers of the vessels were undergoing repairs that this wish might be realized; but with the perversity of fate and contrary to the usual delay in the construction or repair of anything in which Uncle Sam has a hand, said repairs were completed by the 19th, and on the afternoon of the 20th we picked up an unwilling anchor and steamed away towards the city of Foo Chow.

An anchorage for the night of the 23d was made at the mouth of the Min river, and early on the morning of the 24th we proceeded twenty-five miles further, and were forced to anchor again till 1.30 P. M. to await high water for crossing the bar. The entire length of the river as far as we ascended was found an evershifting scene of panoramic beauty. The banks, abounding in nature's green, were thoroughly cultivated, while at several points an opening between the hills disclosed extensive fields of tea or rice. Many Mandarin graves were noticed on both banks, some less conspicuously located, while others still were just in process of excavation. Running along the left bank was a public road having at intervals of several miles curious little wayside shrines. The hills being of a varying elevation and joined by deep ravines, we were often enabled to view the country many miles beyond, and on two occasions the eye encountered what seemed to be a city of greater or less extent compactly built on the summit of a hill, at an elevation of several hundred feet. A high wall of gray stone encompassed the whole, and I have no doubts the inhabitants thereof shook hands with themselves upon their apparent immunity from visitation from French shot and shell. This was, it will be remembered, a time of war; all China was aroused, and every hilltop and situation of vantage had been utilized for purposes of defense; in consequence, rudely constructed forts greeted the eye at every stage of our progress. Guns were belching forth, alarms sounding, flags fluttering in the breeze, and, judging by the extent of such demonstrations, one might imagine that if the French should attempt a nearer approach to Foo Chow, the welcome accorded would be anything but pleasant. Such a showing is, however, merely superficial, and as was demonstrated then and more recently in the little affair with the Japs, China is impotent when confronted by a foe versed in the equipment and practice of modern warfare. We passed a small island in the center of the river which reminded me very much of the Rip Raps in Hampton Roads; this was also utilized as a place of defense, and was rendered picturesquely beautiful by means of leafy trees and abundant shrubbery, which tempered the dim gray of the breastworks and lent an air of romance to any speculation concerning its former use and history. On the occasion of the visit of the French a few months previously, it is said they passed the fortifications and obstructions at the mouth of the river, serenely indifferent to the widely flying missiles of the enemy, and in retaliation for an occasional shot, which, straying away from its companions, came too aggravatingly near, a broadside would be turned loose, carrying death and destruction in its train. One such shot was usually sufficient, as each survivor, regardless of all considerations, felt it his personal and particular duty to make "other arrangements" looking to the well-being of himself.

The result of such exchange of pleasantries might be noticed at intervals along the river in silenced guns and dismantled forts. A few of these were now being rebuilt, and where such was the case an unwonted activity was to be seen. Several of the fortifications destroyed or abandoned, from their positions being so well adapted to defensive operations, would have been adjudged almost impregnable in the hands of other nations. The Chinese government, I think, must ever regret the discontinuing of the policy inaugurated in 1870: that of sending a number of young men abroad each year for military instruction; for by this means modern methods would have been more generally adopted and the army placed on a footing more nearly equal to that of other countries.

The little band of Chinese students who came to this country in that year and were divided among the different military schools and academies exerted a splendid influence in this direction upon their return to their native land a few years later, and during the war with France, as officers of the army and navy, their superior training was abundantly vindicated. During the action near Foo Chow three of these American trained officers bore a conspicuous part, and for feats of bravery and daring were fittingly rewarded with promotion.

We arrived at Pagoda Anchorage on the evening of the 24th, and were welcomed by the *Monocacy*, the little veteran cruiser of the Asiatic Station. This place, which is twelve miles from the city of Foo Chow, takes its name from a large pagoda which stands, solemnly grand, on the summit of a hill, on an island of the same name.

The island itself is about a mile in extent, and perfectly level from its southern point to where the hill begins to rise. A small patch of ground here and there under cultivation, upon which are situated a few miserable native huts, are the only signs of life one sees from shipboard; and, altogether, the prospect of three or four months' stay amid such dreariness was rather disheartening.

At the base of the hill towards the river lay the remains of a fort recently bombarded, its demolished walls and silenced guns bearing indisputable testimony to the effective work of the French. On the other side of the hill may be seen phases of life which leave with the beholder a lasting impression. The monster filth unblushingly lifts its head and looks you squarely in the eye at every turn. At the base of this side, and bordering the river just where it makes a sweeping turn in its descent, are situated a few stores and business places, mostly native. In the course of time the river seems to have encroached upon these so persistently as to make necessary the use of wooden pillars as a means of support. The floors of these shanties were of the plainest boards, and had been laid with spaces between each of at least half an inch, through which the water might be plainly seen coursing sluggishly along. This in itself would seem a splendid vehicle for distributing contagions, and when it is considered that the place is made a repository for all kinds of refuse, the prospects for the people being healthy would appear exceedingly small.

The scenery at the Anchorage is extremely picturesque. Mountains abound, arranging themselves in two circles, an outer and inner, both of which from a central observation seem complete. The sides of these have been furrowed to a considerable height by the hand of the farmer, and the soil from a distance appears extremely fertile and rich. Nearly abreast of where the *Juniata* lay, and directly opposite the pagoda, stands the custom house, and this vicinity is known as the "Custom House Side." There is no wharf or landing of any kind at this point, the place as yet not having reached such a state of importance, and the smooth, sandy beach does service in this respect.

Christmas day, which comes to the major part of

civilized humanity as a day of celebration and rejoicing, found the crew of the *Juniata* imbued with the necessary feeling and impulse, but lacking in the conditions necessary to carry out its usual form of observance. The day was kept as a holiday, and quite a number accepted invitations to share the more elaborate fare of the boys aboard the *Monocacy*.

The caterers of the officers' messes, with their stewards, busied themselves with the preparation of an attractive menu, and as the captain was to be the honored guest at the ward-room feast, the entire ship's resources were taxed, and such meagre supplies as could be obtained ashore were utilized for the event. Several men were early sent ashore in quest of greenery to be used in decorating the ward-room, and with the artistic use of the national colors deftly draped about the skylight and bulkheads, the banquet hall was rendered worthy of both the season and occasion.

The men were generously remembered through each officer looking after the members of his division.

Various kinds of liquid refreshments, with cigars, were sent forward with compliments, and thoroughly enjoyed amid joking, music, and dancing. The steward, Louis, and I had a dinner party to ourselves in the pantry, which took place about the time set for the big affair below.

The spread was neither so choice nor elaborate as that laid before our rival diners, and embraced a stew of oysters, a choice cut of salt pork, and minced meat pies, compounded from the steward's own recipe, out of such ingredients as were obtainable aboard ship; and, though slightly weak in one essential particular, were found extremely palatable; and later, when William remembered us with a bowl of spiced punch, there was thought to be very little remaining that we could reasonably desire. The day closed with a hearty wish on the part of all that the next Christmas might find us among the dear ones at home.

During the first days of our stay here the monotony was somewhat relieved by occasional visitors from Foo Chow, and the Chinese compradores, sampan people, and soapstone venders who besieged the ship at meal-time were a constant source of diversion. These latter would make their appearance even in the most miserable weather, which, with fog, rain, and mist, and chilling winds, would last weeks at a time, until "Foo Chow weather" came to be looked upon as typical of all that was disagreeable and nasty.

Our mail came quite regularly, and this was, of course, a source of expectation and pleasure.

There were also vessels of various kinds coming and going all the while, and we felt to be, at least, not entirely cut off from the rest of humanity; later, however, when the river was blockaded on account of the anticipated attack by the French, commerce received a check, and the absence of these accustomed sights was keenly felt. During this period of enforced quiet and seclusion we found ourselves the objects of the prayerful solicitation of the foreign missionaries stationed at Foo Chow.

Sunday was looked forward to with a great degree

of interest by both officers and men, and when, on account of the particularly bad weather, they were compelled to forego their visit, the day seemed all the more dismal for the disappointment. The little band of Christians, which numbered seven, included three ladies, and at each service an amount of religious feeling was developed which found expression in fervent prayers, voices raised in songs of devotion, and the presence of that indefinable feeling of worship which evidences a current of spiritual electricity reaching out and connecting humanity with its unseen Maker. The exercises, which were held on the berth deck, usually lasted an hour and a half, and at their conclusion the missionaries would be entertained by the officers at luncheon. A rather curious fact was noticed in connection with the missionaries' efforts, that when the gentlemen came unaccompanied by the ladies there were very few officers in attendance on the services, although this fact is, perhaps, not entirely a fair gauge of their piety.

It is difficult to convey to the reader even a partial idea of the depressing dreariness with which one day now followed another with snail-like fleetness. Each twenty-four hours were exactly like the preceding in their even succession of regular duties, unmarked by any important or interesting event.

We turned out at four bells (6 A. M.), and a survey from the foc'sle disclosed the same rugged hills, usually clothed in mist, the gray pagoda, gaunt and ghostly in its somber morning robes, and the dark, murky river rolling heavily along, splashing the ship's sides with chilling monotony, and tossing from wave to wave the little sampans, which laboriously made their way from shore to ship.

The advancing day brought its regular tasks of drill or ship work when the weather was auspicious, and when not, the symbol of recreation, the smoking lamp, sent forth its flickering flame, and with smoking, lounging, sewing, or reading, a comfortable snooze in the seclusion of the berth deck or an occasional tramp on the foc'sle clad in reefer and sou'-wester, filled in Jack's hours until night approached.

The nights seemed interminably long. The men had supper at eight bells (4 P. M.), lamps and lanterns were lighted at two bells (5 P. M.), and for several hours dancing and singing to the music of the sailor's favorite accompaniment, the accordeon, held the deck. The waltz was readily the dance preferred, and the popular melody which inspired its votaries to trip the "nimble" ran in these words:

> "Mary Ann McLaughlin, don't you sigh,
> Take that tear-drop from your eye,
> Don't you let the little ones hear you cry,
> For we'll be married bye and bye."

The time hung no less heavily upon the officers; the day having passed, their leisure evening hours were spent at cribbage or some other chosen game, while the more studious, in the effort to increase their knowledge along special lines, would, in the seclusion of their stateroom, become oblivious to the friendly between-shuffle chatter of their mates until called away by duty or urged by approaching drowsiness to accept the friendly embrace of slumber. My own leisure was chiefly employed in writing up a "log" of the cruise and in reading of a miscellaneous character. Often, however, for entire days the weakened condition of my eyes did not admit of their too steady use, and at such times it was difficult to banish a most oppressive sense of isolation. We were frequently joined in the pantry during the long winter evenings by William, and the hours, beguiled of tedium by song and story or the sweet music of C——'s guitar, would quickly pass and bring us to that season where all conditions of unpleasantness become lost in the realm of forgetfulness. The time spent on light literature might surely have been used to better advantage on matter of a more solid nature, but considering the many dark and dreary days and the total absence of all pleasure, it is scarcely a matter for surprise that one should almost constantly have recourse to that world of fancy and speculation which is so potent in lifting one, as it were, out of himself and helping him to lose for a while, by absorption in the portrayal of other scenes and characters, the vivid consciousness of the depths of his own personal unhappiness.

From Diary, January 23d. The Chinese are busy with preparations for their New Year's, which is the 25th. At this time, as at a similar time with other nations, there is a general adjustment of affairs, and here, those who can possibly do so, go home to worship at the shrine of their ancestors. Last night there was a continuous firing of crackers and cannon, and the air was made noisy, if not melodious, by a variety of Chinese musical instruments.

February 15th. This being my birthday, C——

suggested that we go ashore and celebrate it as best we might. It having been nearly two months since the pleasure of being on land was ours I readily agreed, and, with the captain's permission, we went off about one o'clock.

The day was clear and windy, and after wandering here and there inspecting the ruins of the fort and taking a nearer view of the pagoda, we repaired to the compradores and opened several "cold bottles" (of beer) in honor of the occasion. The place in which we found ourselves was, with its dirt floor and unplastered walls, more like a kennel than the business house of a prosperous merchant, but we were there in the interest of the celebration and did not intend that the primitive quality of our surroundings should mar the pleasure of the occasion.

We accordingly "set to" with our old-time vigor, and with jumping, leap-frog, rope-climbing, and boxing, contrived to spend the time most pleasantly, and paid for it during several succeeding days with swollen limbs and aching muscles. That night in the solitude of the pantry, C——, having gone forward for a smoke, very serious thoughts came to me while reviewing the twenty-two years of my life and endeavoring to form some idea of what my future should be. A few short years ago — a youth; to-day — a man. Youth and manhood, what a world of thoughts in these two words, the former symbolical of that season which ignores the dull cares of existence, when life viewed through the doubtful lens of inexperience, clothes all its pursuits in the beautiful garb of virtuous actions. No sorrows, howe'er severe, suffice to dampen the buoyancy of this, the chief period of natural happiness; then, indeed, is life a series of rose-colored dreams from which the succession of years awakes us too soon,— a heart-rending affliction, an inopportune step which carries grief in its train, and we leave this delightful happiness as far in the distance as though the lapse of years had intervened; we find ourselves men, the beautiful gold of hope which enveloped our youth has given place to the sombre hues of mature reflection; the little cares, which cast but a fleeting shadow along our path, are magnified by quickened susceptibility to the proportion of ever-threatening clouds, while supported by an all-powerful belief in the peace that is enduring as eternity, we plod on through after years toward that abode where we hope to enjoy a perpetual spring of youth and happiness.

CHAPTER XIII.

FOO CHOW AND SHANGHAI.

" Most cities we have honored with a visit,
   Have shown themselves in some things deficit,
But each and all attracted somehow,
   Save that slimy, oozy, dirty Foo Chow."

MOST persons have felt in their lives the deep lively pleasure caused by the anticipation of some coveted and promised enjoyment. As a boy living in the country, sharing only in its natural, innocent pleasures and having only a confused visionary knowledge of the great busy city which lies beyond, feels upon the near propect of a visit to the same, so the writer felt after having been shut up on shipboard for nearly four months and reveling at length in the promise of a visit to the great city of Foo Chow.

Saturday, the 4th of April, '85, dawned bright and clear. The sun in robes of crimson arose in majesty from his western couch, touched mountain and valley and flowing stream with the sparkle of his radiance and gave promise of a perfect day.

Our ship, by virtue of a spring attire of fresh paint and dint of hard scrubbing and cleaning, presented a most cheerful appearance, and as we steamed away in the little launch, with the captain and several officers, there was no one but felt proud of the gallant *Juniata*. The first objects attracting our attention were the arsenal and dock-yard, snugly ensconced within a pretty bayou of almost miniature dimensions.

At the former the red triangular flags of the fort were fluttering in the breeze, and now and then we caught a glimpse of a Chinese soldier clad in their quaintly ugly uniform.

At the latter there seemed to be no work in progress, and if it were not for a half-completed ram lying at the edge of the water, and upon which there were several men at work, the entire place would have appeared deserted.

As we were running up against the tide, sampans innumerable passed us, moving swiftly and bearing each its abundant freight of squalid humanity.

Many of the occupants of these boats appeared miserable in the extreme. The sun by this time was nearing its zenith, and these people, some of them totally unprotected, were sweltering in its rays.

The women and men were generally attired in patches, the former sculling, and the latter busying themselves in some lighter occupation. The children, of which merchandise each sampan has a full quota, were mostly clothed in their birthday suits, and as we passed gazed in wide-eyed wonder. The scenery along the river was above the average, and mostly of a rugged character, with mountains now and then towering to lofty heights on either side, and ever and anon developing some fancy shape. Owing to the sinuosities of the channel, and having low water, we were compelled to make frequent detours, one of which brought us into the Pass of Kimpai.

We here found several junks moored, ready to be sunk at a moment's notice in case the French should pass the lower forts, thus impeding their further progress. During this time the gentlemen in the cabin of the launch whiled away the time with social converse, enlivened by amusing reminiscences from one or another of their number. There were not many complaints of heat, as there was an awning of ample dimensions spread, which, together with the slight breeze induced by the rapid motion of our boat, made the ride quite pleasant. On emerging from the pass and arriving opposite the fort, three of the guns belched forth in rapid succession, and had they been loaded with other than salute charges, I am persuaded this writing would have been done in a vastly different situation. We soon found, however, that the firing was in honor of a mandarin who, with his suite, was approaching the fort on a visit of inspection.

Further along we saw coolies at work, knee deep in mire, with which they loaded their boats and conveyed to some place of deposit. As the river was quite narrow here, it was presumed that they were thereby extending its banks.

It was near here we encountered a scene that made all who saw blush and turn away, and confirmed the writer in the belief that modesty is not one of the prize virtues of the Chinese.

Looking out past numerous junks loading and

unloading, the songs of the natives, which may have been to them merry, falling monotonously on our ear, our vision encountered the city of Foo Chow.

To the left and immediately overlooking the water was a grand pagoda, towering to the clouds, and seemingly well aware of the important functions with which Chinese superstition has invested it. Entering the harbor thronged with hundreds of junks, great and small, and made more hideous by paint of many colors, we reached the wharf of Hedge & Company, and were landed after a ride of something over an hour.

The time was now noon, and the sampan people were all engaged with their midday meal. Stepping ashore with one of the crew of the launch who knew the town quite well, having made the trip several times, we started off to see the sights. I must confess that I had not walked a hundred yards before the buoyancy of the morning with which I had been animated had entirely disappeared, and in its place I felt an uncontrollable disgust. This feeling came partly from the pain experienced in my feet, for they, having been more than three months accustomed to the freedom of easy-going deck shoes, were expressing their indignation at the sudden constraint of a tighter fit. Walking down the first street after leaving the wharf, we were set upon by a couple of Chinese dogs, which, by the way, are the most viciously ugly brutes I have ever seen. We, however, got rid of them by the force of boot leather persuasion, which sent them howling down the street, creating any amount of commotion among the busy throng along the narrow thoroughfare.

The street through which we now passed was built up with a series of little shops, in some of which, in a partially nude condition, were different tradesmen busily engaged at their work. In front of several little eating establishments, set out on a stand after the manner of a fruit stall, appeared several stone jars, containing articles of food, such as pickled dog's legs, boiled cat livers, and other choice and delicious viands intended as an enticement to the Chinese palate.

As a rule, I believe these people approach nearest the Icelander in their love for fat or grease of some sort. We passed several bake shops, their cakes and other eatables exposed on trays in front, and in which the grease glistened with heartburn effect.

After threading many streets of this class, and stepping aside now and again to allow the passing of a laborer bearing his burden in basket scales, we in due time arrived at the extensive establishment of the rich Chinese merchant, Mr. Hok Lee. This was a very large business place, consisting of three floors laden with goods of all descriptions. There were a dozen or more Chinese salesmen, some of whom spoke English tolerably, and one young American, who served the house in the capacity of bookkeeper.

It was said that the immense variety of costly goods seen here, and which were very indifferently displayed when contrasted with the artistic excellence of arrangement attained in similar mammoth concerns in Western cities, represented a cash value of nearly a million dollars. After purchasing some cigars and inspecting any quantity of rare and costly curios, we set out again in another direction. Harris, the young man with me, proposed that we go to the "Sailors' Rest" for a short while. A Chinese city is very much of a puzzle in its windings and unexpected turns, and the stranger without a guide often finds himself greatly confused, and it is just possible that had it not been for my companion a searching party might have found service in rounding up the *Juniata's* cabin boy. Our way took us past the tomb of a mandarin located on the slope of a hill near the suburb. This was of very curious shape, ascending with the hill; it was hollowed out to a considerable extent, its outer rim shaped very much like a mule's shoe, and edged with a heavy coping of gray stone.

The steps leading to the immediate entrance way were broad and of the same material, while against the wall in front of the heavy door stood a shrine at which there was one person at this time paying his devotions. A short distance to the rear of this hill stood the house we were seeking, and, arriving there, found a delightfully cool and cozy retreat.

The establishment was in charge of an English-speaking Chinaman, having a variety of small refreshments and cigars, which he sold at a reasonable price, while a second and larger room adjoining was fitted up for reading, and on its tables we found many late copies of different newspapers and periodicals.

We had now been the greater part of three hours in a burning sun, and felt, in consequence, a trifle uncomfortable; being the only visitors at this hour, and, assuring ourselves no ladies were expected, we proceeded to be comfortable, each in his own way, while looking over the illustrated papers and puffing our cigars, which we found very good manillas.

When thoroughly rested, and having prevailed upon the Chinaman to sell us a few of the older papers for our shipmates, I asked Harris to conduct me to a barber shop where I might have my hair trimmed.

The little native artist looked very much puzzled when he understood what was required of him, for, whatever may be, I know that the "crowning glory" of man was not in this particular instance his hair, for that which does duty in the way of adornment and protection of my cephaloidal extremity has been very inelegantly termed "wool" in the descriptive list of my enlistment papers. It was, therefore, clearly evident to at least the one most concerned that this operator had no adequate idea of the relative value of this class of raw material.

After seating me upon a little tripod, having lavatory and other attachments, he looked at the "stuff" with an expression of complete bewilderment, and finally ran one hand over, rather than through it.

This he repeated several times, inspecting his palm now and then, probably to assure himself as to its harmlessness, and then, with a huge pair of clippers, set to work.

Acting on the principle that a bad job were best done quickly, he had finished in about ten minutes and turned me loose a veritable prince of scarecrows, or, one might have thought my head a pictorial illustration of the hills and valleys of the dark continent. My companion and I had both developed by this time something of an appetite, and, not relishing Chinese cookery, returned to the launch for a luncheon. An evidence of the excitement of the morning, incidental to the preparations for the trip, is found in the fact that I had left behind a lunch that C—— had prepared for me, so that I was compelled to accept a share of Harris' beefsteak, bread, and coffee, which he generously offered me. There was now nearly an hour remaining before the time set for our return to the ship, and this we passed in executing a few commissions for the boys, such as the purchase of sewing materials, stationery, and smoking articles, and a visit to a photographer's establishment, whose collection of native views was most interesting, and detained us until within a few minutes of five o'clock, barely allowing time to reach the wharf. The officers all arrive punctually, the American consul accompanying the captain for a few days' visit to the ship, and we were soon on our way home.

Many persons will wonder at my calling a ship "home," but if they could see it with poor Jack's eyes they would know that the majority of sailors have none but this, and seldom wish another.

The return trip had nothing unusual to mark it; we ran down with the tide, and were all aboard, hungry and tired, by five bells.

On Monday, the 6th, the captain made a trip to the city, and arranged for the services of a pilot to take us down the river on the morrow.

This action was thoroughly discussed in all parts of the ship, and was generally regarded as significant and as the initial step looking to our speedy departure for home. The thought that we were about to make a move looking to this end was peculiarly gratifying, and induced a corresponding elevation of spirits, which became almost uncontrollable that evening when it was learned the *Enterprise* had already arrived in the lower river for our relief.

Tuesday, the 7th, was cloudy and disagreeable, but no amount of bad weather could suffice to dampen the deep pleasure experienced in leaving this miserable place; the pilot came aboard at 12 o'clock, "all hands" were called to "unmoor ship," and at 1 o'clock we were under way down the river.

We were brought to an anchor about four o'clock, just five miles from where the *Enterprise* lay on the other side of the blockade. The captain ran down to her in the steam launch, and on his return said that he would not be able to take the ship through until the afternoon of the 9th.

At five o'clock that day we picked up anchor, and began to move slowly towards the obstructions; every one recognized the vital nature of the undertaking, and all precautions were taken to insure the instant discharge of the pilot's orders. The pilot, captain, and navigator were alone on the foc'sle, word was passed commanding absolute quiet about the deck, and two of the ablest and most trusted seamen placed at the wheel.

The utmost care and skill were necessary to carry us safely through, for between torpedoes and the ship on either side was a margin of a very few feet, so that if she failed to answer the helm at the proper moment, our destruction would have been certain. It may then be understood with what intense interest the few seconds were fraught which were requisite for our passage. The ship's company, battery, and all heavy portable material were collected forward to lighten her aft; not a sound was heard, save that from the engines and the pilot, who directed every movement, and as the final obstruction was passed in safety there was heard a simultaneous sigh of relief, which in its expressiveness may be considered as near a fervent "Thank God," as men of the sea usually approach.

We anchored near the *Enterprise* for the night, and early on the morning of the 10th ran down to Matsui and anchored about nine o'clock within hailing distance of the *Trenton*. Admiral Davis, who had not been in robust health for some time, concluded to transfer his flag to the *Juniata*, and go with her as far as Shanghai, in the hope that by escaping for a time from the oppressive fogs and miasmic vapors of the inland regions he might speedily regain his usual good health.

The transfer of the admiral, with a retinue of four Chinese servants and sixteen musicians, comprising the band of the flag ship, was completed by eleven o'clock, and at eleven forty-five, to the familiar strains of Auld Lang Syne we parted company from the *Trenton*, and bore away at full speed towards Shanghai.

The unexpected arrival of so many strangers created quite a stir among our crew, and a few days passed before we became accustomed to the new order of things. A band of music was a very welcome innovation just at this stage, for our spirits, having sunk so low during our recent exile, needed something more inspiring than the plain old morning and evening "chestnuts" of the bugler.

We now had music, and good music, too, at least twice a day; the foc'sle dancers capered each evening with an increased sprightliness, and for a time the erstwhile melodious accordeon was powerless to charm. Whatever of inconvenience may have been occasioned by this influx of strangers was, perhaps, felt more keenly by C—— and myself, for there were piled in upon us in our little pantry the four oriental attendants of the admiral, and inside of three days they had made every available space a repository for tooth brushes, face-rags, canvas stockings, and other personal effects, so that it was almost impossible to get hold of table requisites without a search warrant.

They knew their business, however, to a nicety, and the perfect and even smoothness of their manner was equaled only by the delightful Mayonnaise of their capable little steward.

Ah Quin, the steward, was a particularly bright fellow, and in his excellent company many pleasant hours were passed ashore, while, before parting finally, he insisted that we have our photos taken together, in memory of our enjoyable acquaintance.

The period from the 14th of April, when we again anchored within the harbor of Shanghai, until the 20th of May, was replete with pleasure as well as events of a more or less interesting nature.

First in importance was the *Juniata's* final inspection, which was held on the 17th. The day was all that could be desired, and knowing this to be our last exhibition while on the station, no efforts were spared to maintain the former standard of excellence, while at its conclusion genuine pleasure was felt at having passed so successfully the last of these trying ordeals.

A great deal of attention was now given to the purchase of clothes and curios, for an outlay on the former represented a decided saving upon the price of similar goods in America.

The Chinese merchant is enabled, through the advantage of a low tariff with England, to offer decided bargains in woolen and cotton fabrics, and the officers and men of the *Juniata* were not slow to see the wisdom of increasing their official or civilian wardrobe at a saving of thirty or forty per cent. The Chinese tailors are also very expert with the needle, and are such perfect imitators that, saving a few details of finish, their work bears favorable comparison with that of the purveyors of fashion in European or American capitals.

Wednesday, the 22d, is memorable as the date of one of those remarkable dispensations of Providence, which suddenly and with appaling effect are wit-

nessed occasionally among the human family. It was just after the noon hour when the men on watch had been sent aloft to furl sail, and having completed their work were about to "lay down," that Riley, captain of fore-top, while stepping from the rigging into the top, missed his footing and was hurled to the deck, a distance of at least thirty feet. The boys rushed to him on the instant, found him breathing faintly, and with tender, loving hands, bore him to the sick-bay below. He was there carefully laid on a mattress, but before the two surgeons were able to do anything for his relief, a spasm was noticed to pass through his frame, a smile of consciousness lighted for a moment his pallid features, and poor Riley's last cruise was done.

The officers of the ward-room were seated at dinner when this terrible accident occurred, and the body, striking the deck with a peculiar deadened thud, was distinctly heard in every part of the ship. On the instant an officer seated at table, with an unaccountable prescience remarked "That is a man fallen from aloft." They each and all hastened on deck and found a horrible realization of the truth of the remark. Our ship was now an abode of mourning, the claims of duty and pleasure and preparations in anticipation of the homeward start were all swallowed in an intensely human and brotherly grief.

Brave and fearless lads, to whom the deadly violence of wind and storm came only as an incentive to heroic exertions, were pale, powerless, and (who knows) perhaps, prayerful in the presence of the majestic sovereignty of death.

The next day, the 23d, witnessed the last scene of this tragic event. The crews of the *Juniata* and *Monocacy*, numbering more than three hundred, followed the remains ashore and formed an imposing procession towards the Catholic church, where a short and solemn service was held, and finally to the cemetery beyond the city.

A cloth-covered casket, about which was draped the Stars and Stripes, and the whole literally buried beneath the floral tributes of his mates, contained all that was mortal of our recent companion. All hearts went out in sympathy for the poor widowed mother watching for this boy in the lonely home at the other side of the world, whose heart had but begun to heal from the cruel wound inflicted by the civil war, and now it needs must be freshly torn. May we not believe that a merciful Father prepared her for this great affliction and enabled her to span the chasm of despair with the hope of a blessed and immortal reunion on the other side.

The news that we were to take the admiral back to Nagasaki to meet the *Trenton*, and that we should receive our orders there, was current in the ship about the first of May, and some disappointment was felt, as many believed that we should start homeward from Shanghai.

A few days before leaving, C—— and I had the pleasure of meeting Mr. George Butler, a gentlemen of color, and one of the substantial citizens of this thriving port. He was a native of Baltimore, the son of a minister of that city, and had gone out to China in a merchant vessel during the war; his splendid native ability and general business qualifications soon won for him merited recognition, and at the time of our visit the distinction was his to represent as general manager one of the largest ship lines in the East. Mr. Butler, at his demise, several years ago, was the possessor of a snug fortune, and was survived by his wife, an estimable lady of European birth, and two children.

Monday, the 18th, was the date of the last of a series of receptions given by the officers of the *Juniata* to the "four hundred" of Shanghai.

The ship was gaily decorated for the occasion, and the whole of the after part above and below decks was utilized in the entertainment of the numerous guests. The amiable wife of Lieut. Richard Rush, who, with their charming young daughter, Miss Daisy Rush, was then traveling in the Orient, very happily performed the duties of hostess. A canvas screen was stretched amidships abaft the smokestack, while an awning, affording a pleasant shade, spanned the quarter-deck, and with the sides enclosed by bunting of different colors, made an attractive ballroom of generous size. The guests began to arrive at four o'clock, and from that hour until after six was witnessed a scene in which sweet music, the graceful dance, lovely women and gallant men formed a charming ensemble of life and gaiety.

A most genuine and hearty regret seems to have been the general feeling as our final visit to Shanghai drew rapidly to a close, for in and around this oriental metropolis, more than all others, there are to be met many pleasing phases common to the life of western cities. One is not here left entirely to the mercies of purely native associations, for as the novelty and charm of these wear away, the pleasure may be his to mingle with people more nearly akin, if not of his immediate nationality.

The crew, as well as the officers of the *Juniata*, during a number of visits, had each in their sphere drawn to them a large circle of acquaintances, and in many instances these had developed the warmest friendships. It is not suprising, then, in view of the uncertainties of life and the immense distance to be traveled, that a more than usual interest should attach to this leave-taking. The ship was dropped ten miles down the river at four o'clock on the afternoon of the 19th in order to clear the bar at high water and be ready to leave early next morning. This distance, however, furnished no barrier to a few of the younger officers who had perhaps engaged to spend the last hours ashore, and, notwithstanding they were obliged to depend on the native sampans to bring them off, they bravely took all chances.

The result of this was that at 1 o'clock A. M. they had all found their way aboard, with one exception. In pursuance of the admiral's orders, we got under way at four o'clock, and just as we had given up hope of the missing officer reaching the ship, a lusty halloa came to us from up the river, and after a few moments of waiting a sampan dashed alongside, and there clambered aboard Lieutenant ——. This was truly a hairbreadth escape, and I hope and trust the poor sampan man was well paid for his successful exertions.

The admiral was very indignant at this lapse of discipline on the part of the offending officers, and for their tardiness, as well as unmistakable evidence of a genuine parting "sorrow" which accompanied them aboard, they were sentenced to enjoy the solitary delights of the ward-room for five days.

Sunday, May 24th, was rather a dismal day aboard the *Juniata*. Extremely cloudy weather, a heavy sea, and a rate of speed not exceeding three knots per hour were but little conducive to the elevation of the spirits of a set of men whose watchword now was home and friends.

Some amusement, however, was afforded the crew just after the dinner hour by the antics of our pet cat "Bob," in his fruitless efforts to catch the many birds flying about the ship. A few of the men also exhibited their feline attainments in this direction, and one of them by crawling out on the foretopmast yardarm was successful in catching a beautiful pelican. The fact that a great many different species of birds that are not supposed to travel beyond a certain distance from shore were now our constant company was abundant proof, if such were needed, that we were traveling close to land. Many of these feathered creatures seemed extremely tame, and one particularly so flew in through the cabin skylight while the admiral and captain were at dinner, and was made a prisoner by the latter. Our other two birds were placed in a cage together, and the stranger installed in a little home of his own. He seemed quite cheerful during the day, but imprisonment proved too great a burden for his rugged, roving spirit, and the next morning we found him cold and stiff on the floor of his cage.

As the day advanced, a thick gray mist made its appearance on the horizon, and, spreading rapidly, we were soon within the circle of its sombre shadow. Steam was meanwhile put on, and every possible precaution usual in such cases was taken. An additional lookout was stationed at the cat-head, the bell regularly tolled, and the hands at the wheel doubled. It was expected that we should make a certain lighthouse about eight o'clock, and at the proper time a light was reported; but, on investigation, no one but the lookout who had so reported could make it out.

We then ran on at about six knots an hour for about thirty minutes. The situation now was one of deep interest; the mystery of the reported light, to the sight of which the lookout still firmly adhered, made prominent the thought that we might be nearer one of those rocky islands which abound along this coast than was generally supposed. The monotonous ding-dong of the bell, and the even song-like tones, at regular intervals, of the man heaving the lead, in their ceaseless iteration, formed a medley of ghostly sounds which added to the general and natural feeling of uneasiness.

No movable light of any description was allowed about deck, while the foc'sle was occupied exclusively by the captain, navigator, and officer of the deck. It was about 8.30 that the voice of the lookout rang through the ship in startling tones, " Land ahead, sir! Dead ahead!" The navigator seemed to see it at the same time, and immediately put the ship under "one bell," and after a short interval "backed her."

As seen from the bow, the land upon which we had so nearly run appeared a huge boulder, shelving gradually into the sea, and standing forth in dull black, though clearly-defined proportions, within a setting of grayish mist and vapor. So near were we to it that it seemed, by putting forth a hand, we might actually touch it.

The mist had been absolutely impenetrable, and its being lifted just in time to save us from going to pieces seemed little short of providential.

After steaming backward a considerable distance, we again went ahead slowly, and were finally brought up to the proper course.

The heavy fog, so nearly fatal to us, had entirely disappeared when the early watch was called next morning, and the captain, before turning in (he had remained on deck all night), left orders with the officer in charge to send her ahead at full speed, which resulted in our being safely at anchor at 10 A. M., on the 25th, within the beautiful waters of Nagasaki Bay.

We found the many ships in harbor gaily dressed with flags and bunting in honor of the Queen of England's birthday, and as soon as an anchorage was reached our men were put to work to show similar courtesy and appreciation for so auspicious an event. The admiral, captain, and flag-lieutenant then set off in the "barge" to make official calls, and at 12 o'clock every vessel of war took part in a general demonstration of twenty-four guns salute in honor of the day.

The other American vessels in port were the *Ossipee* and *Alert*, the captains of which were early aboard to pay their official respects to the admiral. Her majesty's flagship *Audacious* fired a salute of sixteen guns on the morning of the 26th with the American flag at the fore in honor of our admiral; her sails had been loosed for the purpose of drying, as likewise the other ships in harbor, and, whether through oversight of their officer of the deck or some other reason, the salute was fired without furling. The opportunity to give a practical lesson in naval courtesy was not lost on those in charge of the *Juniata*, and, after our sails had been made neat and trim, a return salute to Britain's flag was fired.

In anticipation of an early start by the *Juniata* for America, the admiral caused various sessions of courts-martial to be convened on the different vessels for the purpose of clearing up the business of the fleet. The trial of Lieutenant W—— of the *Alert* for drunkenness was held aboard the *Ossipee*, continuing three days, and resulted in a suspension on furlough pay for two years without loss of rank; he was also ordered to report to the *Juniata* for passage home. Another session was convened aboard the *Juniata*, on May 30th, for the trial of Sheridan, a fireman, for jumping the ship; he was found guilty and sentenced to a year's imprisonment in one of the penitentiaries of the United States; he also was given passage in the *Juniata*. On June 7th a general transfer of men was made; those having a long time to serve were sent to ships that would remain the longest on the station, while those whose enlistment would expire within a few months were sent to the *Juniata* for passage home. The invalids and court-martial prisoners were also consigned to our ship, so that it was much feared the capacity of the ship would be greatly strained during the long voyage homeward.

Monday, the 22d, at noon, the *Trenton* steamed into harbor, and, upon a signal, took a position two ship lengths from the *Juniata*. During the dinner hour the band played a special program in honor of the approaching return of the admiral's flag to the *Trenton*, concluding very appropriately and effectively with "Home, Sweet Home."

About four o'clock the Chinese attendants, with the staff baggage, left the ship, and it was with genuine regret that we parted from the steward, Ah Quin, who had been found companionable and a thorough little gentleman in every respect.

The commander-in-chief, with staff, took an official leave at 5.15, and to the officers of the *Juniata* assembled on the quarter-deck he said that his stay had been most pleasant as well as of great benefit to his health.

All of us were sorry to lose the music of the band, and especially so were the dancers, who were thus once more thrown upon the good offices of their faithful friend, the accordeon.

The spirit of rivalry between the crews of the second gigs, which had been growing since the coming together of so many American vessels, culminated in a series of interesting events which took place on the 25th, 26th, and 27th.

The course was straight, and extended three miles from the mouth of the bay, past the bow of the *Ossipee*, which marked the goal.

Each day, as the hour for the races approached, the rigging and tops of the many vessels appeared black with human forms, and hundreds of sampans were hired at advanced rates for the occasion, while the shore was well lined with native and foreign spectators. Our boys worked faithfully, but were not equal to the superior training of the *Trenton's* crew, who were accorded the championship. The winners becomingly celebrated the event on Saturday evening, the 27th, with a dinner at the "Trenton House,"* at which the vanquished were the invited guests.

The remaining days of our stay at Nagasaki were employed in preparations of a general nature looking to our departure on the 1st of July.

The social pulse, as might be expected, was perceptibly quickened, and this was evidenced by quite a number of enjoyable events both aboard and on shore.

Our crew was allowed an opportunity to give the Japs a parting whirl during the 28th and 29th, which they did right royally and in good shape, and at the

---

* This house was named after the flagship *Trenton*, and was owned and operated by a colored man, an old man-of-wars man by the name of Johnson, who had been in Japan eighteen years. He was married to a Japanese woman, by whom he had one son, a handsome boy then sixteen years of age.

proper time, without an exception, returned aboard ready and impatient to begin the homeward voyage.

C—— and I spent the afternoon of our last day ashore, and, on our way down to come off to the ship, we looked across the harbor to where the *Juniata* lay, and were greatly pleased to see flying from the mainmast, with a graceful sweep over the mizzen and stooping to kiss the waters at the stern, the emblem for which we had looked and yearned many weary months — the homeward bound pennant. This long, narrow streamer of parti-colored bunting is purchased by the crew of each vessel about to leave for home, and the day when it shall be "broken" is looked forward to with delight by all on board. The one in question was ordered and made in Shanghai eight months previously, and had been safely stowed away until the period of its usefulness should come. All hands were early astir on the morning of the 1st, and by nine o'clock the general preparations for sea were completed.

The captain paid a parting visit to the admiral and returned aboard at 9.30, when we immediately got under way. The tour of the harbor was made in becoming style and with our streamer, 250 feet long, flutteringly describing the most beautiful curves, the men in the rigging waving caps, cheering, and being cheered by the American, Japanese, English, and Austrian war vessels.

As we steamed past the *Trenton* a hearty goodbye was sent up from four hundred throats, the band played "Home, Sweet Home," while the admiral and officers bade us *bon voyage* from the upper deck. When about a mile down the bay the American flag was hoisted to the fore and a parting salute to the admiral was fired, which, with the response, was caught up and re-echoed from the hillside and borne to our ears in friendly tones of final farewell.

CHAPTER XIV.

ACROSS THE INDIAN OCEAN.

A RATHER disagreeable passage of fifty-six hours brought us to the wharf at the Arsenal, twelve miles below Shanghai, where we had been ordered to exchange a piece of equipment with the *Ossipee*. The transfer was made without delay, and at 4.40 on the morning of the 6th we were again under way down the coast bound for Hong Kong. A stop was made near Sharp Peak, where the U. S. S. *Enterprise* awaited us. This vessel was also homeward bound, but was to proceed by way of Australia, while our orders carried us by way of the east coast of Africa and the Cape of Good Hope.

Our business with the *Enterprise* detained us but a few hours, and after an exchange of many hearty cheers and waving of caps, we held away on our course.

Our stay at Hong Kong, where we arrived on the night of the 12th, was made as short as possible, on account of the cholera which was then raging with much virulence.

The captain had intended giving the men "liberty," as this was the last desirable port for that purpose we should reach before arriving at Cape Town, three months later. The *Juniata* was here deprived of one of her officers, Lieutenant Mitchell, who had been in poor health for some time, and it was thought the discomforts incident to nearly five months of almost constant travel would prove too great a strain in his weakened condition.

He took passage on the steamer leaving Hong Kong on the 17th, and returned to America, by way of Europe.

The captain, as well as his brother officers, deplored losing so companionable and efficient an officer.

We left here at 7 o'clock, on the evening of the 16th, for Singapore, carrying an extra supply of coal on deck in sacks to avoid any unnecessary delay for want of fuel.

The season of the much-dreaded typhoon was now approaching, and no precaution was neglected, looking to the placing of the ship in a condition whereby she might be immediately and properly handled in case of an emergency. These precautions were, however, to no purpose, as the weather, during the eleven days' run, was all that could be desired, except on the night of the 23d, when, with a stiff wind and a high sea we rolled considerably. It was about four bells (2 A. M.) that I was awakened from a deep sleep by a blow on the head and the sense of something wet and disagreeable pouring over my face; for a second, being somewhat stunned by the blow, I imagined all sorts of things, and after a while becoming sufficiently awake, I knew that the last violent roll of the ship had dislodged the inkstand from where I had insecurely left it the evening before. I may add, the cabin lantern and mirror disclosed to me a view of myself I had never seen before, and even now, an occasional view of my old navy blanket with its ink-spots furnishes a hearty laugh in remembrance of my very ridiculous appearance in the quiet of that early morning.

We arrived off the island of Singapore at 11 P. M., Sunday, the 26th, and anchored within the harbor at 9 A. M., the 27th. On the 29th, we again took the bitter pill of coaling ship and had an extra supply in sacks as formerly.

This was the most filthy of our experiences; whether or not the coal was softer or handled more carelessly, I know not, but the cabin quarters, which in every particular were tightly closed (as the captain spent the day ashore), were found at the conclusion of the process to be almost as deeply in mourning as any other part of the ship. Our two little Chinese canaries, when they were at length brought out in the sunlight, and given fresh water, could only whistle in husky tones, and in seeming rebuke for such harsh treatment, their notes sounded very suspiciously like "Down in the coal mines, underneath the ground," etc.

Leaving Singapore at 9 A. M. on the morning of the 30th, we headed for Zanzibar, proceeding by way of Straits of Banca and Sunda.

A splendid breeze sprung up during the afternoon, steam was knocked off and sail made, under which we bowled along for two days at a speed of eight knots.

The morning of the 1st of August found us in a dead calm and we again went ahead under steam.

At Ange Point, the headland of Java, off which we arrived at 9 A. M., Sunday, the 2d, we found several sailing vessels waiting patiently for a breeze to carry them through the straits. We "lay to" here the greater part of the morning and took advantage of the opportunity to send mail ashore.

The skipper of the bark *Edward May* of Boston, one of the becalmed vessels, hailed us and said he was 105 days out from New York, was bound for Hong Kong, and that he had been here four days trying to get through the straits. He asked the captain for an American newspaper, saying he had not seen one since leaving home.

Quite a bundle was made up for him, and learning we were homeward bound, said he was very sorry he couldn't go along with us.

There was here also a Portuguese brig in charge of her second-mate, the captain and first-mate having been swept overboard in a gale off the Horn. Ange Point is an extremely desolate looking place, and the captain, who was here in '82 on his way out with the *Juniata*, said he could notice very little, if any, improvement. That was but a short while after the eruption of Krakatoa, at which time most of the northwest portion of the island of Java was submerged. A few native huts scattered over the low, even soil were now the only visible evidences of habitation. Before leaving at noon, several boat loads of natives came off with fruit and fowl and found eager purchasers in the caterers of the different messes.

The captain said at luncheon that we would soon have a look at the volcano that caused so much trouble a few years ago. Its outlines were first seen in the distance about one o'clock, and two hours later a perfect view was had. It took the shape of an elongated cone; smoke was still pouring from its crater and, at the distance of eight miles, numerous and deep gorges, through which the burning lava had poured, were plainly visible to the naked eye. It is said that the effects of this memorable display of nature's forces were distinctly felt several thousand miles away at the extreme southern point of Africa.

The trip upon which we were now started was to be the longest yet experienced; about 4,500 miles lay between us and Zanzibar, and various estimates were made as to the time in which it should probably be completed. Continuing our way we had soon left Krakatoa far behind and were now fairly at sea.

The equator was crossed without a perceptible "jarring" of any kind, and the wind, which at first was light, came out strong on the afternoon of the 8th, and steering S.S.W., we, in a short time, caught the "trades" on our port quarter, the fires were ordered banked, and we proceeded under sail, making an average of over 200 miles per day.

We found the weather now very warm, but not uncomfortably so, except to the prisoners or invalids who were obliged to remain the greater portion of the time in the stuffy atmosphere of the berth-deck. The former were allowed an hour's exercise on deck under a sentry's charge each afternoon.

The forward part of the ship for more than ten days had the appearance of a menagerie, from the different animals and poultry which were being carried along in pens or running loose at will, to be utilized in the supply of provisions when the fresh meats should be exhausted. The number of these were steadily reduced after the first week, and on the 20th, the last of the live stock, a very funny little pig that had become a great favorite and had been named Jerry by the men, was very regretfully offered up as a sacrifice.

As our course took us out of the usual line of travel we were the greater part of the time alone on the wide, wide sea, without so much as the sight of a sail; but during the entire passage there was no complaint of an oppressive sense of loneliness; on the contrary, the minds of all were employed with speculations as to the future, and the general trend of the usual conversation about deck would seem to indicate that the realization of these prospects was at best but a few days distant rather than several months away, and, even so, contingent upon making a safe voyage over thousands of miles of oceans.

The conditions, however, in which we were placed were such as could only inspire hope; the weather continued good, we were making excellent progress, and a welcome relaxation from the steady routine maintained on the station gave the men an abundance of time in which to sew, read, or amuse themselves. These twenty-three days were particularly enjoyed by myself, much of the time being passed on deck within the shadow of the great foresail with a book as companion, or more often an interested observer of the different forms of marine life passing before me from time to time. Aside from numerous fish of a smaller size which were easily lured to the surface, by casting overboard any remnant from the table, much amusement was afforded by the very lively actions of an occasional school of porpoises, which during several days traveled along at the head of the ship, tumbling with a queer side-wheel motion from wave to wave or indulging in a free for all scramble for whatever might be thrown them.

Several expert anglers among the crew occupied their leisure hours very successfully with rod and line, and through this means furnished a welcome variety to the general fare, which towards the end of the trip had become restricted to the one item, "pork and beans" — baked, boiled, and sometimes cold.

On the 20th the hands were put to work scraping masts and yards, painting ship, and in every way removing the effects incident to the long passage which was now rapidly drawing to a close. About three o'clock on the afternoon of the 23d the outline of Zanzibar was seen in the distance; and, steaming on past numerous small islands and coral reefs, the ship was brought to an anchorage at 5.30 o'clock about a mile from the city.

The city of Zanzibar, built on an island of the same name, had an estimated population in 1885 of

120,000, more than half of whom were Arabs, and the remainder divided between negroes, Madagascans, and East Indians. The town is made up of a number of irregular, narrow streets, usually very dirty, except in front of the harbor, where are located the palace of the Sultan and many business houses. As may be supposed, being in about the sixth degree of south latitude, we found the weather uncomfortably hot, and were accordingly well pleased that our stay was to be of short duration. The native negroes, however, with bared feet and a costume no less brief than picturesque, paraded the burning sands in seeming indifference to the torrid heat.

The dress of the men consisted of a long white muslin gown reaching nearly to the ground and a red skull cap. The clothing of the women was arranged in two sections, one of which was a piece of colored stuff reaching below the knee, while the other, a cotton scarf of fancy colors, red being most conspicuous, was worn around their shoulders, and partially covered the bosom. No covering was worn on the head except the hair, which was decidedly short and harsh, but this in all cases they had found a means of plaiting, and generally looked quite neat. The heads of the Madagascan women were covered with suits of heavy, dark, lustrous hair, and presented generally a much more comely appearance than their sisters of African birth. All were alike, however, in their taste for a profusion of jewelry, mostly silver and brass, which in a variety of strange designs was worn in their ears, through their noses, and on their toes. The eyes of the native women were encircled by a thin ring of soot, which was said to indicate a tribe, without reference to state as single or married. They were of much larger physique than the men, and impressed one with the idea of strength and endurance rather than grace and tenderness. From an exhibition of brawn and muscle in which I saw one of these ebonized Amazonians indulge, at the expense of her undersized lord and master, I am persuaded a proper and becoming respect is insisted on by these ladies of Junoistic proportions. Their color varies between a chestnut brown and a stovepipe black, more often the latter. A considerable traffic is maintained between the interior and coast towns by East Indian merchants, who employ agents to travel back and forth to purchase or exchange articles of clothing, provisions, and other merchandise.

In the course of a conversation with Mr. Pereira, one of the leading merchants, he mentioned the fact that a journey inland by any one unknown to the native tribes generally ends in death inflicted in a barbarous manner, and for the traveler in European clothes the most cruel tortures await. We visited several pawnshops and African bazaars; in the former were seen all kinds of native trinkets, some of considerable value, but gotten up in the most extraordinary designs and settings. There were shown us also many different implements of war, from the small silver-sheathed dagger usually worn by the chiefs of clans or tribes to the huge broad-pointed spear or javelin used by warriors both in battle and for the chase. In the bazaars we were shown various little native curios, such as jewelry made from the gum tree, fans and mats of peacocks' feathers, and canes made from the elephant's hide, which were wonderfully tough and elastic. The proprietors of these places were Arabs, who are usually accounted very shrewd men of business. The native houses are mostly flat-roofed and built of stone. The outer walls are plastered and whitewashed, while within the bare beams are exposed, and, with floors of hardened dirt, the whole appears extremely dingy and unattractive.

The Sultan's palace, which is situated on the edge of the bay, and only a few minutes' walk from the main landing, is a large stone building of regular appearance, and is, perhaps, more solid and comfortable than architecturally beautiful. Immediately in front, and standing in an open space or park, is a lighthouse built of stone, and towering to the height of 200 feet.

One evening during our stay, when we were about to come off to the ship at ten o'clock, we noticed great crowds of persons, chiefly Arabs, wending their way towards the palace. The street or avenue in which the Sultan's residence is situated was brilliantly luminous with lanterns and torches. Deciding not to go off until we had learned the meaning of so much display, we walked along this street until we came to the public place; here the scene of the avenue was repeated, and, perhaps, the illuminations were even more brilliant. The lighthouse standing in the center appeared a huge shaft of fire; thousands of natives, both Arab and African, in a costume of pure white and red turbans, were promenading and jostling each other good-naturedly, while puffing their cigarettes, laughing, talking, and enjoying themselves generally.

Sweet strains of music ravished our ears continually, and at intervals we were surprised to hear celebrated selections from fashionable operas rendered with pleasing and artistic effect.

Lights beamed brightly from every window of the palace, and, approaching the great entrance, we found seated on either side the uniformed guard of the Sultan.

We were determined to see as much as possible, and taking on a most important bearing, and trusting to the powerful magic of our foreign uniforms, admittance was granted us without question, and, gaining the inner hall, found ourselves confronted by a squad of forty or fifty soldiers. We here made known by signs to one who appeared to be in charge our desire to see the palace, who motioned us to stand where we were while he inquired. When he had left, the excitement to a near approach to royalty wearing off, a look about us disclosed a large and well appointed waiting-room, upon the walls of which were many implements of war, arranged in various designs, while immediately opposite the doorway stood a magnificent mirror in a frame of bronze and reaching from floor to ceiling. A massive staircase of excellently polished ebony led to the upper floor, and in front of the landing above was placed another large mirror, at the base of which were gracefully banked a variety of beautiful plants. This was as far as our gaze was permitted to extend, for at this moment the official returned and gave us to understand that our presence was not desired. He then directed us out by way of the court in which the musicians were stationed, where an Arab attendant, who spoke English fluently and seemed quite communicative, informed us that the Sultan was giving a dinner to the German Naval officers.

The band, composed of several nationalities, numbered a hundred performers, and were divided in two sections, one relieving the other, and so affording constant entertainment. The scene here was one of interest and great beauty; the court was without cover save that of the starry heavens, and in the center the waters of an artfully constructed fountain fell incessantly with a refreshingly cool and pleasant murmur.

The air was filled with the aroma of sweet plants, and these, the gems of the tropics, might be seen along the balconies in luxuriant profusion. I, however, could not help thinking, notwithstanding all these pleasing associations, that the greatest element of beauty and adornment was wanting — woman; so it is that she, who is the foremost consideration among people of other civilizations, has here only a position of minor and degraded importance. We were further informed that the Sultan was in possession of over 200 concubines and one legal wife; and passing a portion of the harem in which these women live, there were noticed on an upper veranda, in a stooping position, many forms peering through the railing in rapt contemplation of the scene below.

They were only allowed to exercise at a certain

time in the garden of the palace, and taken occasionally in a close carriage for a drive in the country, attended by a detail of the Sultan's guard.

We got off to the ship about twelve o'clock, and before turning in witnessed an elaborate display of fireworks, with which demonstration the Sultan closed his evening.

The *Juniata* took coal aboard on the 26th, and on the evening of the 27th a start was made for the little island of Johanna.

CHAPTER XV.

MOZAMBIQUE AND MADAGASCAR.

THE "Comoros" are a group of volcanic islands, made up of Johanna, Angaziya, Mayotta, and Mohilla, and lying in the Mozambique channel, between Africa and the northwest coast of Madagascar.

As we approached this little group, the gems of the Mozambique, early on the morning of the 31st, the eye, by contrast with the heated sands and low coast line so recently left, was filled with a view of lofty hills, densely clothed with trees of giant growth, so thickly mingled as to appear an almost solid mass of intertwining leaves and branches.

An occasional space, cleared for cultivation, shows a soil of unusual richness, growing the chief source of the island's wealth — the sugar cane; or affording luxurious pastorage to numerous herds of splendid cattle. The scene is delightfully refreshing. No element is wanting to emphasize the general aspect of entire peacefulness. The waters of the smallest lake to which the surge and roll of angry waves are never known, could not be more beautifully calm than the venerable "father of waters" on this quiet August morning. The glorious sunlight in an unbroken sheen of dazzling brightness spread over the sea, far and near, and with a pleasant sense of restfulness the vision turned to the tranquil beauties of the harbor near at hand.

The impression gained by a first sight of the city of Johanna, and, indeed, that which strengthens with familiarity, is of its evident antiquity. The houses, few and scattered, are of heavy gray stone, and picturesquely built amid surrounding trees at various elevations along the mountain side. There are the remains of an old fort, commanding a view of the harbor from the height of a thousand feet, and flying the Sultan's colors in token of his complete dominion over the island.

The *Juniata* had been ordered here to adjust differences between the Sultan and Dr. Wilson, formerly a resident of the United States, in a dispute growing out of an extensive tract of land thereabouts, upon which the doctor, by grant of the Sultan, was cultivating sugar very successfully. An effort to extort an exorbitant tax was the cause of the trouble.

This matter detained us more than a week, which was not particularly pleasant in view of a natural desire to hasten homeward.

A duly organized court of inquiry was convened in the cabin during several days, with the Sultan, his two sons and nephew, and a numerous retinue *vs.* Dr. Wilson, in regular attendance. The Sultan was a man of medium stature, and apparently about sixty years of age.

Time had taken from his face the rich Arab tint and frosted his hair and beard and overhanging brows. His eyes, dark and deep set, still retained a gleam of their wonted fire, and glanced here and there with restless watchfulness; a scarf, fresh and white, deftly coiled about his brow, was in perfect tone with the snowy purity of his graceful robes, and completed a figure of regal stateliness and dignity.

Two sessions were held each day, with an intermission at 12 o'clock for luncheon. As per the captain's orders, the steward had prepared coffee and a generous supply of tongue and ham sandwiches for the first day, but when they were handed around each Arab guest shook his head in courteous though firm rejection.

Coffee they accepted and greatly enjoyed, but would have none of the sandwiches. Said Jaffra, the Sultan's nephew, who acted as interpreter, in explaining the circumstance, said that the tenets of Mohammed taught them they would be defiled should they partake of animal food not killed in a certain way, viz.: with the accompanying ceremony of prayer and ointment. Cake they consented to eat only when assured by the captain that it was made with butter and not lard.

Said Jaffra, unlike the others, who were in native Arab dress, was clad in a neatly-fitting uniform of European make, with gold braid plentifully displayed on coat and trousers. A Turkish cap covered his head.

A somewhat heated session was held towards the close of the trial, when considerable feeling developed among the attendant Arabs through the doctor, in a fit of temper, applying to the Sultan the epithets *thief and liar.*

Nearly all were reduced to tears, and made known in broken accents how it grieved them to have one they loved so much called such names. They threatened to leave the ship at once, and were only persuaded to stay after the doctor had retracted his words and on the captain's assurance that nothing of the kind should occur again. Business was here suspended for a season, during which the recent ill-humor was puffed away on deck with the smoke from their cigars.

On Sunday, the 6th of September, an incident happened which drew the interest and attention of all on board. About seven o'clock, while the usual early morning work was in progress, I was startled by the officer of the deck singing out, "Let him come aboard." I looked out of the pantry port immediately, and on the deck of the steam launch which was alongside being cleaned by her crew, there stood a young African, apparently eighteen years of age, chilled and dripping with the water from which he had just emerged.

He was evidently very much afraid, and, on the approach of the men, made a motion to spring again into the water. Upon seeing, however, their intention was friendly, he allowed them to bring him on board.

He was placed in care of the master-at-arms and conducted forward, where clothing and food were given him, as well as an opportunity for repose. An hour later the men had christened him very appropriately Johanna Sunday. The captain was made acquainted with the event, and about three o'clock he had an interpreter from ashore find out something of his history.

The interview was conducted in the cabin, the boy kneeling on the deck between the captain and interpreter.

He told his story with true natural oratory; his voice, rich and sweet, was made more impressive by gestures which came without an effort, while his countenance portrayed the deep emotion which shook his frame.

At the close of his narrative he joined his hands before him in an attitude of petition, and thus remained while it was being interpreted. As gathered from the interpreter, he was one of the king's slaves, and had been a witness to a murder committed on the island about six weeks previously, and, fearing that the guilt in some way might attach to himself, had fled to the mountains and had lived, the companion of birds and animals, during the following weeks.

At length, early on this Sunday morning, he had seen a strange vessel from his mountain retreat, and determined to swim to her, a distance of at least a mile and a half, for protection. After this interview Johanna soon became thoroughly at home among the men, joining in their games, and doing chores about the ship. Everyone was interested in him, and it had been determined long since, in the councils of the foc'sle, that the proper thing would be to bring him to America with us. On Monday night he did a native dance to the music of his own voice, surrounded by both officers and men, and it would seem from his evident enjoyment that this was the happiest moment of his life. At the session of the court next day Johanna was brought before the Sultan's people, and all said they did not know him; yet, strange to say, the captain received a letter from the Sultan that night claiming the boy as his slave. Whether or not Johanna got wind of the Sultan's claim, or life aboard ship had become distasteful, we probably shall never know; but the fact remains that a search of the ship on Wednesday morning failed to reveal our Johanna. He had vanished; dropped overboard and swam ashore during the night, perhaps; and so he slipped out of our life as silently and mysteriously as a few hours before he had come into it.

The adjustment of affairs on the island was satisfactorily completed on the 9th of September, at which time the doctor sent aboard as a compliment to the crew several hundred pounds of sugar, besides a large quantity of vegetables, fruit, and a huge bullock. He stayed aboard ship that night, and went with us next morning around the coast to Pamoni, from which place we sailed at two o'clock the same afternoon for Mayotta.

MAYOTTA.

This island, the second in size and the first in importance of the Comoro group, is one of the French colonies, and the administration of affairs is in the hands of a governor.

The inhabitants are chiefly Arab and African, with a few families of colonial settlers. There is no slavery here, which fact alone is sufficient to make it admirable. A number of small islands, green and beautiful, meet the eye at different points, and an occasional hamlet of six or a dozen diminutive stone dwellings may be seen peacefully clustered in a spot at once romantic and beautiful.

A small fort, mounting twelve guns, which answered our salute to the Governor, is built at a point commanding the harbor entrance. The place, as a whole, looks clean, fertile, and prosperous, and to that extent attests the presence of foreign influences. Left here at 1 P. M. Saturday, the 12th, for Majunga.

MAJUNGA.

A run of twenty-four hours brought us to the above-named town, situated on Bembatooka Bay, on the northwest coast of Madagascar.

This is considered the most important port on the island, although the different consular representatives usually reside at Tamatave, on the east coast. The French have also gotten a foothold here, and have erected a fort almost before there are any possessions to defend. The day being Sunday, there were no salutes fired. Three or four vessels flying the French colors were the only other ships in port.

Our stay here was very brief. Whatever of business had made the trip necessary was completed by five o'clock, and in as short a time as the anchor could be gotten up we were speeding almost directly across the channel for

MOZAMBIQUE.

A most delightful run brought us within sight of the city at three o'clock on the afternoon of the 15th, and five o'clock found us anchored within the bay. We had quite a joke on the steward the day before, who, in utilizing for dessert a portion of the fruit from Johanna, had instructed the cook to boil one of the species, which was about the size of a good head of cabbage. Of course, after this process it was reduced to rather an uninviting mush, and when served the captain said it was a very delicious custard apple, which simply required cutting in half and to be eaten with a spoon.

The territory of Mozambique extends from Cape Delgado, on the north, to Delagoa Bay, on the south. The capital, Mozambique, is built on a coral island, facing an extensive bay, which affords excellent harbor facilities. The Portuguese, who are the nominal owners of this tract, have built up the city as a convict settlement, and through this means the population has developed a mixture of Arab, African, and Portuguese, with any number of half-castes, who might with propriety claim almost any race. The affairs of the settlement are under the control of a governor and staff. Slavery, which was formerly carried on openly, and latterly with the occasional connivance of the government officials, is still known to some extent.

The captain had intended staying here only two or three days, but found several matters that required his attention, as well as important instructions from the department, which made a longer stay necessary. I was ashore two or three times, and should have enjoyed the visits very much had it not been that the heat was almost intolerable. In such circumstances, a pleasant position under an awning on deck, where a delightful breeze always stirred, was far more enjoyable. On Sunday, the 20th, in company with Sharp, one of the ward-room boys, five or six hours were spent ashore, during which a visit was made to the business place of Mr. Auerbachs, a German Jew, and former resident of Boston. He did a sort of general merchandise trade, and had the most extensive business at Mozambique. It was partly in his interest that the *Juniata* was here detained.

The streets of the city are narrow, and the houses, built of brick and stone, are all painted a white, red, or yellow color, and seem to gather the rays of the sun as effectively as do the sands which burn through your shoes and glisten upon you at every turn. We occupied about two hours of our time on this Sabbath afternoon with a visit to the fort, which, with the barracks and prison quarters, is situated at the harbor end of the principal street or avenue.

This walk is splendidly shaded from where it connects with the more thickly-settled portion of the town along its entire length, and reaches out over the narrow strip to the point occupied by the fort. The sea may be seen on either side rolling on a splendid beach, sometimes noisily, as if in anger, and again, with a gentle playful motion, chasing successive waves far up on the whitened sands.

Several natives were noticed along the beach engaged in gathering shells, coral, and sponges left exposed by the receding surf, and on our return we were fortunate in finding some nice pieces, a few of which now serve as souvenirs of that far-off coast. The fort is a quadrangular-shaped structure built of stone that had once been gray, but was now more nearly black through contact with the heat and storms of more than two centuries.

Its otherwise even outline is broken by abutments and embrasures made necessary for the better training of its cannon and by the exigencies of location. There are eighty ancient guns mounted throughout the fort, and no doubt these were considered a most effectual armament in the days of its early existence. Around the guard-house just within the massive gates where the sentry patrolled his beat lounged a number of soldiers, smoking, talking, or sleeping away the idle moments. Within the enclosure the various office buildings, together with the prisons, or rather pens, of the convicts, fences, and, in fact, everything save the trees, which are whitewashed, have been painted a very disagreeable yellow, and under the influence of a scorching sun has a most unpleasant effect upon the eye. The grounds in other respects are made attractive with beds of flowers and neatly-kept gravel paths.

The pens of the prisoners were arranged in a row at either side of the square or open court. A full-length iron grating ran along the front of each and tallied more with what we had seen in use in menageries as cages for wild animals than the places in which human beings should be confined. They were about 8x10 feet in size, and within this narrow space there were confined as many as eight persons.

There were a few chained hand and foot, and all in a state of semi-nudity. Seated on the ground in front of one of the pens was a most pitiable object; he was entirely without clothes, and was performing in an abstracted manner a most repulsive operation.

We afterwards learned that he was suffering from a species of dementia, was very docile, and had been allowed to do pretty much as he pleased within the grounds. Some of the pens were supplied with a few conveniences, such as tables, chairs, and beds, while the occupants were allowed to move about unfettered. They were all Africans, and one young fellow, who spoke a little English, asked us for a smoke. We handed him a cigar through the bars, and, after lighting, he strutted back and forth the length of the cell with the airs of a peacock, and excited a general and hearty laugh among his fellow prisoners.

Wearying of these sights we returned to town, and, after some refreshments at Auerbachs, sallied forth again, and by taking another route came to a different section, which we found more thickly settled by the native Arab and African races.

The latter, in their costumes and physique, were much the same as those seen at Zanzibar, while in their manner, voice, and general demeanor, they resembled a large class of Afro-Americans, found occasionally in the north and east of the States, but in greater numbers at the southland. We encountered several groups of women and men who gazed at us with wide-opened eyes and a good-natured grin, and who would pay their respects to us after we had passed by a shrill "He! He!" or a profound "Haw! Haw!" The town was policed by Africans clad in brass-buttoned black jackets, sack-cloth trousers, and white helmets. They paraded their sandy beats with much dignity, and would stop on their rounds to whisper something sweet to some dark-skinned belle, or at a convenient moment step aside for a mouthful of refreshments to renew their sun-stricken spirits.

Near the water front at this end is situated the market-place. The business of the day was long since over, and under its broad roof a welcome shade and cool retreat were found.

It was a low-roofed, rambling structure, having pillars of stone, with the exception of which the place was entirely open on all sides.

There were gathered here in different attitudes quite a number of natives of both sexes, sitting or reclining at pleasure, laughing and talking; the sea breaking with a musical roar almost at their feet, and the whole forming a ideal picture of indolent ease that can never be forgotten. Our last hour before going aboard ship was spent on the seashore, sometimes with bared feet wading along in the surf or plodding through the sands. We were not alone by any means, and among others we passed an Arab, within whose hour-glass the sands of time were running low, and as, with his hands clapsed behind him, he trod with feeble step the heavy beach, he seemed to look beyond the shining waters to another and more distant world. So intent were we in our rambling, and so completely under the influence of the strange and almost weird sublimity of the locality, that we reached the landing too late for the launch, and were obliged to wait for the next boat an hour later. During this interval I purchased from a young Arab a neat little cigar case made of straw and prettily mounted with different colored beads.

Monday, the 21st, the Governor paid an official visit to the ship, and was received by the captain and officers in full dress and a "battalion present." A salute of seventeen guns was fired on his departure, with the flag of Portugal at the fore, which was returned by twenty-one guns, with the Stars and Stripes waving over the fort.

The process of coaling ship, always a disagreeable and unwelcome operation, was here delayed until the day before leaving port. The poor, half-naked Africans who, under an overseer, toiled from early dawn till the going down of the sun, presented a most pitiful picture of the effects of "man's inhumanity to man." The institution of slavery, though abolished through international mediation, still flourishes along this eastern coast, and its resultant evils are readily apparent in the abject sloth and degradation of the long-suffering blacks, as well as by evidences of the most outrageously brutal treatment.

All of these coalers were branded in one way or another, while several were hideously disfigured. One great fellow of giant size had his brow burnt in ridges from one eyebrow tip to the other, and the entire front of another's body was seared in such a manner as to resemble the proof of some ancient writing.

The poor fellows furnished much amusement for the men, who played with them in much the same way they did with "Jakey" and "Billy," the pet monkey and dog of the ship.

Several of the berth-deck cooks, when clearing up their mess cloth after dinner, threw bones and other remnants among them, which they almost fought for, and greedily ate, coal dirt and all. No end of jokes were played upon them, and one fellow, whose legs were very long, was persuaded to don an old uniform belonging to a sailor whose legs were extremely short; his hair and face were filled with flour, and, the trousers striking just below the knee, made a figure extremely ridiculous, and caused much merriment among the men about deck. The coalers, however, took everything good-naturedly, and rather seemed to enjoy being in such jovial company.

Our stay at Mozambique came to an end on the afternoon of the 23d, when we picked up anchor to recross the channel for another visit to Madagascar.

Early on the afternoon of the 25th we arrived off Maevarano, a name which dignifies an assemblage of a dozen or more primitive dwellings on the Malagassy coast, at about sixteen degrees south latitude. Mr. Smith, the American agent, as well as the commercial representative of Roper & Co. of Boston, came off to the ship, and spent several hours with the captain and officers.

He was clad in a suit of white duck, with cap of

the same material. His feet bare, and trousers rolled above the knee, were more in keeping with the rolling surf and a shallow canoe than a well-appointed cabin; but, in listening to his amusing anecdotes, many of which related to his personal experiences in the island, and interesting accounts of some of the curious customs of its inhabitants, one readily lost sight of all defects of apparel. In his case the dress certainly did not make the man. The matter of our stopping here was not due to any special or important business, but was, perhaps, traceable to a well-defined scheme of governmental diplomacy, by which it is sought by all great powers to instill and foster a feeling of respect and confidence, and so conduce to the civil and commercial advantage of all concerned. The captain had quite an assortment of home papers and other reading matter gotten together from the ward-room and steerage, which Mr. Smith gladly accepted with the remark that there was nothing he could have received that would have given him so much pleasure.

He left the ship at 7.30, and anchor was immediately gotten up for Morundava.

Mr. Stanwood, the American agent here, came aboard soon after our arrival on the afternoon of the 26th. He was engaged in conversation with the captain during several hours on general matters; was persuaded to partake of the latter's hospitality in the way of dinner, and was finally comfortably bunked for the night in the port state-room.

Monday, the 28th, the Governor of the province, with his aid, and escorted by the American agent, paid an official visit to the ship, and was received with the same honors accorded the Governor of Mozambique. He was clothed in a semi-military costume, consisting of frock coat with brass buttons, black trousers, and cloth cap trimmed with gold braid. His manner was at once easy and dignified, while his English, spoken with a rather engaging accent, was at once refined and scholarly. I could not but regret, while listening to his interesting remarks concerning the island, that the people he so ably represented should by their long drawn out strife and contention between the two ruling factions, the Hovas and Sakalavas, render their influence as a nation abortive, and so greatly impede the gradual progress of the state towards a higher plane of civilization, where she might take a commanding position among the nations of the earth. Certain it is that while the country is thus in a constant strife and turmoil, and its energies weakened and misdirected, any decided and effective advancement is impossible, and at the same time a shining mark is offered for the display of "annexation" traits in the character make-up of other more powerful governments.

France and England have long since been aware of the advantage to be derived from an acquisition of Madagascan territory; foreign flags have for years fluttered defiantly from the forts of invaders along its fertile shores, and it is easily credible that the spirit of conquest is in no sense satisfied, and the signs of the times even now indicate that preparations are under way for the laying of violent hands on some other portion of her splendid domain.

Madagascar may, however, consider herself reasonably free from spoliation at the hands of America, for, as a rule, the diplomacy of our republic prefers to exercise its powers on game a little nearer at hand.

After looking over the ship, the visitors partook of some light refreshments, and, when leaving, I was commissioned by the captain to accompany them as the bearer of an assortment of canned fruits for the Governor's wife, who was in rather delicate health.

In this relation the services of Dr. Woods, the ship's surgeon, were also tendered and accepted. We were all taken off in the second cutter, and when about half a mile from shore were transferred to a surf boat, from which we were in a short time landed on the beach.

The Governor was here met by a squad of twenty partially uniformed militia, and escorted to Mr. Stanwood's place, which we found a very neat little cottage, built entirely of reed and the fibers of the cocoa palm. His wife, a comely, pleasant little woman, was in waiting, and seemed quite delighted with the compliment sent by the captain. When our party arrived on the beach for the return trip, we found a lot of pigs, chickens, geese, and several sheep, and a stack of sugar cane to be taken aboard as a parting remembrance from his excellency.

While coming off I found myself in rather close quarters on account of the space required for so much live stock, and, being obliged to sit on the rim of the boat, it is not strange that I was more than once caressed by the playful surf, and found a change of clothing imperatively necessary on arriving aboard.

However, the inconvenience was only trifling, and the cause a worthy one. Mr. Stanwood came aboard at six o'clock to accompany us as far as Tullear Bay, for which port we got under way at seven o'clock.

Since starting from Nagasaki on July 1st, the *Juniata* had covered 9,244 miles, and had been favored with almost continuous good weather. This exceptional record received a check on the present trip, when, after being out but a few hours, we encountered adverse winds and a heavy, rolling sea.

Having been so long accustomed to smooth sailing, it was some time before we could get our sea legs together, and, judging from the way a few of the boys were tumbled about, they must have thrown theirs away altogether.

It seemed too bad that our usually well-mannered ship should behave so outrageously with a visitor aboard, but so it was, and, like a spoiled child, she seemed to choose this occasion to get off her meanest pranks. I am sure Mr. Stanwood wished many times he had remained in his quiet home, for the slightest comfort was impossible at any time either night or day. The cabin table, which had to be screwed to the deck, was aided at meal time with a wooden rack or frame to prevent the dishes from sliding, but in the highly hilarious humor in which the ship now seemed to delight, this was of no advantage, as the dishes themselves seemed to be in an equally riotous mood.

The feat of dining during this passage was accomplished only by a series of surprising and equally ludicrous gymnastics, in which the author's part on one occasion was not entirely without discomfort to at least one of the other performers. The incident occurred in this way: The ship seemed to have reached a climax of abominable rolling just at the dinner hour, at which time the captain, Mr. Stanwood, and two of the ward-room officers were seated at table. Tomato soup was the first course, and, when about to send this in, C—— said that the captain would not be able to manage the tureen, and concluded to serve it from the pantry. I took in each hand a plate of the steaming liquid, watching closely first one and then the other, and, carefully bracing myself backward and forward against the direction of the ship's roll, had almost reached the goal when the roll on which I expected to deliver the goods was cut short by one of those sudden choppy seas, and sent me forward like a shot on the head and shoulders of Mr. S——. Well, you may be sure, matters were very warm around that board for a moment or so, and I immediately pictured myself in the brig with bread and water for a diet. Happily, Mr. S—— was a man of exceeding good nature, and, after the first shock from contact with the hot soup, which I have no doubt was "painful," had passed, treated the matter as a good joke, and led the laugh at his expense. The wreckage was cleared away, and, with great hardship, but no further mishap, the dinner proceeded to a finish.

At 9.30 A. M., October 1st, an anchorage was reached within the broad waters of Tullear Bay, and in a short while the ship was surrounded by a fleet of outriggers loaded with chickens, eggs, pigs, spears, and mats. We had learned some months ago that the dusky natives along the coast had but a faint appreciation of money as a means of purchase, but rather preferred bottles in exchange for their produce. In consequence, each mess had been at great pains since leaving the station to preserve everything of that description. The cabin stock of this medium of exchange amounted to nearly four dozen, and for these we received twelve dozen eggs and several pretty mats. Quite a number of little pigs were bought in the same way by the other messes, and were allowed to roam at pleasure about the decks. The natives here were a very curious looking people, and accurately realized the usual descriptions remembered in the geographies of our early school days.

The captain's business necessitated remaining in port over Friday, the 2d, but the 3d found us again at sea headed for Port Natal, on the southeast African coast. A slight breeze was discovered after leaving port, which, coming from the right direction, was deemed sufficiently strong to warrant the attempt to go under sail. Canvas was spread to the royals, and, the log giving us a speed of five knots, we were well content, especially as the passage would take at least five or six days and coal was now getting low in the bunkers, necessitating economy in this direction. Our wind stayed with us until the third day, when, towards afternoon, it began to fall off, and by night had dwindled to the faintest zephyr. Steam had meanwhile been put on, and we went ahead at slightly increased speed and were reasonably sure of covering the distance of 800 miles by the afternoon of the 8th. The captain had a little dinner party on Sunday, the 4th, at which the guests were seven of the ward-room officers.

The gentlemen were brought together chiefly to sample the "Tullear Terrapin," which was gotten up in C.'s best style, and furnished the "*piece de resistance*" of a menu which included such other choice viands as a baked pig and roasted goose, all of which, from soup to the dessert, a most delightful *soufflé*, was partaken of most heartily.

Calculations regarding the time of our arrival were shown to be quite accurate, for we were again within sight of the African coast shortly before noon of the day named. About this time the sea was rolling heavily, a strong wind came up suddenly from the southeast, while the appearance of the sky, where great piles of heavy black clouds had gathered, ominous and threatening, seemed to indicate that we might yet have a little unpleasantness before reaching an anchorage. Shortly after five o'clock the storm burst with a terrific thunder clap, followed by sharp and fierce flashes of lightning. A few seconds later a violent downpour fell about us lasting several minutes, when gradually the clouds began to lift, and by the time the ship was brought to anchor at 5.30, every vestige of the storm and cloud had passed away, a beautiful bow of promise mirrored itself in broken prisms of delicate color on the surface of the dancing waters, and nature was once more serene, radiant, and smiling.

Our anchorage was at least three miles from the

shore in the open sea. The United States consul came off to the ship next morning in the surf steamer and spent several hours. As there was nothing to detain the ship, and the engineer reporting sufficient coal to carry her through to the Cape, the Captain decided to keep on down the coast to Port Elizabeth, where we arrived at midnight of Sunday, the 11th.

This thriving town, although not so favored as its older rival, Cape Town, is accounted commercially the most important of all South African ports. Its open roadstead, which is regarded suspiciously by all sailing vessels, deprives it of the trade of a large class of merchantmen, who naturally prefer the usually safe and quiet waters of Table Bay.

Its inhabitants are, however, more strictly English than those of the other settlements, and a considerable and exclusive trade is carried on directly with the mother country. A breakwater less than 400 yards in extent affords protection to many vessels of small size, but is totally inadequate to the requirements of an extensive harbor. The city is built on a gradual incline, and at the base of this, Jetty street, the principal thoroughfare, extends for several miles in the direction of the water front, while leading inland along the coast are numerous well-paved smaller streets, upon which are many well-built dwellings of wood or stone. An extensive suburb, throughout which are scattered pretty cottages with beautiful lawns and gardens, has been developed on the more elevated portion, and to the rear of this may be seen the thickly-settled, tented city of the native Kaffirs.

There are, of course, quite a number of natives

within the city, offsprings of the different inland tribes, but the business is almost exclusively in the hands of the English inhabitants.

As may be imagined, it was very gratifying, after so many months of isolation among people of various foreign tongues, to be able to have ourselves understood without having recourse to the language of pantomine. C—— and I enjoyed our little holiday immensely, having left the ship at one o'clock Monday afternoon, with the captain's permission to remain over night, we were enabled to see a great deal of the place, and, during the evening, looked in at an amusement hall, where a great number of Kaffir people were enjoying themselves with music and dancing. A comfortable bed was found at the George Hotel about midnight, and after a refreshing rest, an early return was made aboard ship the following morning. When the crew were "turned to" preparations were immediately made for the run to the Cape. A splendid breeze blew from the northeast, and nine o'clock found us with head pointed southward and tearing through the water under steam and sail at a lively twelve-knot gait, with every heart buoyant with hope and happy in the thought of so soon reaching this long-looked-for point in our voyage homeward.

CHAPTER XVI.

ROUNDING THE CAPE.

THE sun shone out clear on the morning of the 15th, the steady breeze of two days before still held with us, while the waters of the Southern ocean in the vicinity of the Cape, which we were now gradually nearing, presented an endless stretch of foam-capped waves, ever rising and falling in active, noisy motion.

A first view of the green-clad slopes and valleys of the extreme South-African coast brought all hands to the foc'sle, and during the remaining hours until the anchor was dropped in the bay, a delighted lot of scene-gazers crowded the decks.

The leading attraction in the world-famed beauties of this interesting coast was seen about 5 o'clock, when, after a wide sweep to the southward, the ship was gradually brought up, and we stood in towards the shore immediately in front of that wondrous projection of mighty rock known as Table Mountain. Adjoining on the west stands the majestic Lion's Head, solemn-visaged and grand, its lower outline tapering off to seaward and forming a promontory which effectually shelters the harbor from the turbulent waters of the outer sea. As seen from our anchorage in Table Bay the view is one of unexampled beauty and grandeur. The city is spread out over an extensive area at the base of the surrounding mountains, while on the lower elevations in the background may be seen numerous suburban villas charmingly located amid leafy trees and gardens of fruit and flowers.

We had been anchored but a little while when the mail came aboard, which precipitated a general and almost uncontrolable excitement. The master-at-arms, elevated in the center of a set of feverishly anxious men, proceeded to discharge the task of distribution. Most of the matter had been mailed five or six months previously, and had been forwarded from place to place since July 1st, when the ship left Nagasaki. Each little news parcel was, however, gratefully received, and the lucky ones would scuttle away to some obscure corner to quietly devour their latest intelligence. My own mail included two letters from the folks, one from friend H——, informing me that he had again become a prey to the demon of restlessness and was then sheep-raising in New South Wales, and a bundle of Washington *Stars*. These latter furnished C—— and myself with reading matter during the remainder of the voyage and were read and re-read many times, while noting with affectionate interest the many well-remembered places indicated therein. These copies, which soon became soiled and worn, were regarded as priceless treasures, and were never loaned except under solemn promise to be returned the same day. Our stay at the Cape covered eight days, the first three being given to a general overhauling and repairing and the taking on of a plentiful supply of coal, in view of the long passage which lay before us. When matters had been satisfactorily shaped a liberty of forty-eight hours was granted each watch, during which the boys had their last frolic on foreign soil. The magnificent scenery which environs Cape Town is not by any means its only attraction. The city itself presents many features of exceeding interest. The Dutch were at one time in possession, and many quaint and original evidences of their early settlement still remain, while the life and habits of a numerous colony of Dutch and Boer half castes, upon whom English customs are but partially engrafted, afford an ever engaging and amusing study. The buildings are of stone and brick, and the streets, upon which the houses are uniformly built in squares, are broad and generally well-kept. The government house is situated in an extensive park and is connected with the botanical gardens by a public walk of ample size. The Cape has been for some time the chosen center for astronomical investigations in the southern hemisphere and possesses an observatory replete with every known modern equipment. Numerous hotels and restaurants afford excellent accommodations to a large floating population.

A drive inland over the smooth country roads is a pleasure not to be ignored by the visitor, and will always remain a source of delightful reminiscence. A line of street cars traverse the city, while the steam railroad, which runs several hundred miles through the upper country, has contributed its share to the architectural adornment of the city in the shape of a very handsome depot.

Thursday, the 22d, the home-bound pennant again floated from the main, and the crew were radiantly happy in anticipation of the start on the homeward stretch. As the mail-boat was expected during the day, the captain decided to wait until evening for its arrival. At 7 o'clock she had not made her appearance, although the mail signal was flying from the station, and, as we might still be detained some hours, it was decided to make the start.

The boatswain's mate cried "All hands up anchor for home," and at 7.30 we were under way. Coming out of the harbor our way took us past the German flag-ship. The band played one of our national airs. The crew manned the rigging and gave us three hearty cheers, to which we gave fitting response. When about ten miles out the mail steamer was met and it was thought the satisfaction of news from home would more than compensate the slight delay occasioned by returning to port. At 11.15, with mail on board, a final start was made, and the wish often expressed that the last stage of the homeward passage should be as pleasant as the night was beautiful. The sky was cloudless; the sun, though long since withdrawn from sight, had left a halo of delicate coloring which might be faintly traced high in the heavens.

The moon, lustrous and beautiful, and surrounded by myriads of bright gems, shed a soft and mellow light over all, while Table Mountain, with the formidable Lion's Head and shaft-like Devil's Peak on either hand, stood in solemn guardianship. Sleep, which is usually a welcome visitor to poor Jack, on this night came most reluctantly, and when the watch was changed at midnight, the men who had been relieved still lingered about deck, and in subdued tones talked of the Cape and the end of the long cruise which was now but a few weeks distant. The first five days out were most auspicious; the log gave us nearly a thousand miles, the weather was pleasant, and in many ways the ship's temper might be described as distinctly jolly.

One cannot, however, reasonably expect a nine-knot breeze to last indefinitely, and so, when it began to fall off on the 28th, we bore up bravely, knowing that steam was at our command.

A continual diminution of speed was experienced until the afternoon of the 29th, when the best we could do was to struggle along at an abominable three-knot pace, with no prospect of "raising the wind" from any quarter. Hour succeeded hour, and found us with empty, flapping sails, and the same snail-like progress. The captain, hoping that the temporary lull might soon be succeeded by a good wind, delayed putting on steam until the slow progress became even too depressing for his calm temperament; and, to the delight of everyone, when the watch was changed at midnight, the order was sent to the engineer. It was, indeed, a great pleasure to feel again the constant throb and quiver imparted by the mighty power which urged us on, and the ever-recurring thump and thud and ceaseless noises of machinery came to our ears as sweetest music, and inspired a feeling of complete and general satisfaction. It may, of course, be presumed that the captain was as anxious to make a quick trip as any of the crew, and his position, while one of unbounded authority, was one of grave responsibilities.

The passage required many days, and it was impossible that the ship could steam all the way; so that it was of first importance that every available wind be used to conserve the coal supply against storm or accident, or in case the trip should be unavoidably protracted. There were days following when, depending alone on sail and contending against adverse winds, the conditions were such as to make even the most patient the least bit restless.

On one occasion, when the wind and sea seemed leagued against our further progress — when the ship, straining and creaking, was apparently going backward as much as forward — the captain said to me, while making the effort to go through the form of luncheon: "John, don't you ever go to sea again; if you get home this time, stay there," which was accepted at the time as very excellent advice, and such as the following of which would entail no great degree of hardship. I may, however, venture the opinion that the feelings indicated by the captain's remarks are shared by every man of the sea, but they are only temporary, and with a change of weather are replaced by buoyant spirits, an increased loyalty to old King Neptune, and a caressing fondness for the good ship which bears them onward. On Saturday, the 31st of October, at 10 A. M., we arrived off the historical island of St. Helena, whose rugged steeps and fertile groves witnessed the final act in the tragic life of the great Napoleon.

We "lay to" a few miles from shore, and all hands found their way on deck, where, with a passing view, each bore his part in the world's reluctant tribute to the massive brain and iron nerve of him whose history shows the most conspicuous combination of brutality and wizzard-like genius known to any age.

By the aid of the ship's glasses we were enabled to distinguish a few of the most noted features, including the lofty and sombre crags known as "Lot and his wife," and the picturesque mountainous passage called "Hells-gate," which is the entrance to a glorious stretch of meadow-land most inappropriately named the "Devil's Garden." On the right of the little city of Jamestown there ascends to a height of 2,000 feet a mass of uneven rock known as "Ladder Hill," from the lengthy staircase, said to number nearly 700 steps, which rise in a straight line to the summit, upon which are located the fort and signal station. It had been thought the captain would run in here for coal, which would have delayed us at least two days, and much satisfaction was felt when it became apparent that our acquaintance with the famous island would be limited to this brief survey from shipboard.

The fiery spirit of the exiled warrior was scarcely more impatient for liberty to carry out his plans of universal conquest than the crew of the *Juniata* to measure the watery space which separated them from friends and home. Man-of-war's men are usually deeply interested in the time made by the different vessels of the navy in covering any given course. In this relation, it was ascertained from reports, which are conveniently gotten up by the department for ready reference, that the U. S. S. *Essex*, which returned home by this route two years previously, was thirty-four hours behind the time made by the *Juniata* between Cape Town and St. Helena, a distance of about 1,800 miles. Partly by reason of this, the continuance of good weather, and the fair rate of speed being made, the crew were in a most happy frame of mind, and confidently looked forward to a speedy and successful termination of the trip. As if in support of this belief, " Old Wiggins " informed all hands confidentially that the present run counted him a full half-score times around the Cape, and the magic number (10) assured an abundance of luck to all on board.

Sunday, November 1*st*. Weather cloudy and pleasant. Crew were beat to quarters and general muster, after which the smoking lamp was lighted, and the remainder of the day spent according to the individual pleasure. Steam was knocked off during the night, and we are bowling along under sail at seven knots, which is generally looked upon as a vindication of the " Wiggins " prophecy of yesterday.

Tuesday, 3*d, in* 12° *S.* Weather bright and considerably warmer, which is not strange, since each revolution brings us nearer the equator. The ship's company started in to-day on routine drills, so that we may be in good shape for the final inspection. Nothing seems to go hard with the boys now; they know it is for only a little while, and they turn out with as great alacrity for fire quarters at midnight as might be expected in attending the more pleasant operation of feeding.

Thursday, 5th. Wind came out strong during the night, and the tramp, tramp of the watch, the shrill whistle of the boatswain mate, and other discordant sounds incident to handling sail, meaning increased speed and an earlier approach to the beloved shores of America, came to those not on duty as most welcome music. When I came on deck at three bells (5.30), everyone was busy scrubbing and washing clothes. It was washday aboard the homeward-bounder, and the boys, thinking it might be the last, had, with true homely instinct, gathered together every fragment of soiled wearing apparel, which resulted in the lines being thickly strung with a promiscuous assortment of blue and white garments, the arms and legs wildly cavorting in all sorts of frantic motions.

Sunday, 8th. The sun shines fiercely upon the deck, although within the shadow of the sails one finds it very pleasant.

We are speeding along at nearly ten knots, which is doing very well, and it is said by the knowing ones that we owe our excellent progress to the southeast trades, which are the usual hope of mariners steering northward from the cape at this season.

If our good fortune holds, Saturday will place us the other side of the line; another week will find us at Barbadoes, where, it is said, we will run in for coal and provisions, and then, hurrah! for the homeward stretch. The men are busy to-day looking over and airing their stock of curios. Each one has his bag or box on deck, and there is spread out to catch the rays of the sun a variety of articles such as shawls of silk or crape, panel pictures, and native photos; Japanese boxes and vases of china or bamboo; combs, card-cases, and innumerable articles made of tortoise shell; African matting, fans, spears, tomahawks, and beautiful Angora muffs and mats with long, white, silky hair. In addition to these, all are provided with one or more suits of citizens' clothes, which they are at great pains to shake and brush and fold in anticipation of their approaching season of usefulness.

Saturday, 14*th.* Crossed the line about 9 o'clock, in longitude 36° W. The log gives us 206 miles for the twenty-four hours. Steam was put on her during the mid watch of last night, and the latest foc'sle prophecy places us at Barbadoes about the 24th. While C—— and I were seated within the shadow of the great foresail dreamily puffing our pipes and pursuing in rather a lazy way a conversation concerning our prospects after reaching America, Sharp, the colored ward-room boy, approached us with a heavy cloud on his usual smiling face. On inquiring the cause of so much gloominess, he took from his bosom a copy of the North Carolina —————— of the issue of March 6, '85 (two days after President Cleveland's first inauguration), and called our attention to a leader under the significant caption, "Our First Duty." The article contended that the first duty of the administration was to afford relief to those sections of the *staunch* and *ever reliable* South, which, by reason of a large and rapidly growing *nigger* population and the ills resulting from Republican *nigger* proselytizing, had become disagreeable in the extreme as places of residence for self-respecting whites; further, that said *nigger* should be with all possible dispatch relegated to the condition which God and nature intended, and from which an alien sentiment wrested him to advance the interests of a renegade class as against the chivalry and manhood of the noble South, etc., etc.

In such manner did the wrathful editor vent his spleen and voice the unalterable feelings of a set of hide-bound negro-haters, rascally supporters of lynch law, and conscienceless oppressionists.

After reading nearly a column of such fevered nonsense I was no longer unable to account for the troubled brow of our young shipmate, for his vivid imagination already foresaw a very serious curtailment of the rights and privileges of his people. He anticipated a condition of affairs in which might be seen many repulsive features of that institution whose taint sours the milk of kindness in the breast of humanity, and whose fearful blight shall for many years to come prove an unrelenting dragon in the pathway of the aspiring sons of Ham.

I had thought a great deal of the recent change in the controlling element in American politics and its immediate bearing upon the colored race, but until to-day no conception came to me of the "fear and trembling" with which the older and more illiterate would view the altered condition. I asked Sharp if he thought there was any danger of the colored people again being reduced to slavery, to which he replied, "It might not be jest exactly slavery, but them

Demicrats would certainly make it kinder hot and unpleasant." I found it no easy task to disabuse his mind of these impressions and show him that the administration would most probably shape its policy towards the negro in such manner as to eventually eliminate every feeling of anxiety and to attract to the standard of Democracy a considerable share of this growing political factor. I said it would be the surest suicide for the party to maintain any such attitude as the fire-eating editor of this little journal would have it assume, and contrary to that spirit of self-preservation, which is the great forcing pump from whence springs the actions of parties as well as individuals. Besides, the apple of power has been "forbidden fruit" during so many years that every energy will be so directed as to make possible its continued enjoyment, and there can be no surer way of bringing wormwood out of its sweetness than by inaugurating a system of persecution or ill-treatment of the negro.

I concluded by saying there was nothing to fear but all things to hope from the change, and I doubted not but the Democratic mill would grind out as plentiful a crop of foreign ministers, consuls, and federal demigods as even the most enthusiastic could wish.

Thursday, 19*th*. The weather is fearfully warm. Steam was knocked off yesterday, and we now have but little more than three days' fuel in the bunkers. The ship is creeping along in a most aggravating way, with sails flapping and every indication of a steady calm.

The fact that the ship is free from rolling and resting with graceful evenness on the bosom of the water has been turned to good advantage, and in line with the thorough overhauling which has been in progress during several days, the catamaran was rigged over the side this morning, and its crew, in white working-clothes, are industriously brightening up the ship's sides with a coat of fresh paint, the process of scraping the same having previously been accomplished.

All hands are busily engaged with work of some kind, and, as if to conform with the general stir and bustle, the captain has ordered the painter to invade the exclusive precincts of our little pantry, and we find ourselves for the time being in the position of the man who fails to pay his rent — set out of doors.

Monday, 23*d.* How happy we shall all be to get beyond the influence of a burning tropical sun. The nights are usually pleasant, and some relief is afforded from the heat of the day by occasional squalls of rain which strike the ship with but little warning; there suddenly appears in a clear sky a huge bank of rolling clouds, the officer of the deck immediately orders whatever change in the sail and yards he may consider necessary — the skylight and hatch-hoods are thrown over, and before these precautions are well completed everything is drenched by a warm summer rain. These are always refreshing; the men do not mind the soaking in the least, and while it lasts, paddle about with bared feet, keenly appreciative of the sudden change. The sun is soon out again, and in a short while everything is dry and uncomfortable as before.

Thursday, 26th. At length, after nearly a month of sky and water, we are anchored in Carlisle Bay, off the English town of Barbadoes. Fair and of wondrous beauty does this isle appear to us in the early morning light, its verdant hills reaching up to catch the first sparkle of golden sunshine, which, a little later, glances along the lofty spires and over the broad buildings of the city, kisses the dewy leaves of the graceful palm and buries its burning blushes in the deep waters of the quiet harbor.

The ship is soon overrun with natives, both men and women, the former runners for business houses or curio venders, and the latter in search of laundry work, or passing to and fro among the crew with bright smiling faces, their heads covered with kerchiefs of gay colors and offering for sale little jars of Guava jelly, beautifully clear, and, as we soon find, delicious to the taste. The steward's return from market with an abundance of fresh provisions, which after so many days of communion with paymaster's stores are a pleasure simply to look upon — indeed, we are highly pleased with everything we see, and were it not that there is within us a constant yearning for the old familiar scenes and faces so long lost to sight, we should be content to linger for several days, where nature, always munificent, has left her royal impress in a land of unusual beauty and delight. The nearer, however, we approach our beloved shores, the more impatient of all delay, and it is with great satisfaction that we hail the coal ship as she hauls along side shortly before noon. The process of coaling, withal so filthy and disagreeable, is easily tolerated under the circumstances, for concerning this, as all matters of infrequent occurrence, we may say "it is for the last time." C—— and I went ashore with the captain after lunch, who, upon landing, left us to return the visit of the American consul. We first went to the extensive establishment of Dacosta on Broad street, and, after ordering sea stores and provisions, engaged a vehicle and started in for a general overlooking of the town. We visited several large business houses and were surprised to find people of color employed on every hand in positions of responsibility, and performing easily and well their various duties as clerks, accountants, cashiers, or salesmen. Several large concerns were owned and managed exclusively by colored men, and I was informed that representatives of the race held numerous positions of honor and emolument under the government.

So far as I am able to judge from what I see of them here, and know of them in the States, the features of character which distinguish the Barbadian from the American negro are his spirit of self-dependence and a just and absolute faith in the equality of his manhood, which is shown on all occasions, whether business or social, by a manner at once easy, graceful, and natural. The reason for this difference may probably be found in the fact that there is scarcely a person living on the island who was old enough at the time of the general emancipation in 1834 to remember anything of the debasing effects of a system out of which manhood must inevitably come, bruised, bleeding, and subdued. The act of

England did its work effectually and for all time, and has needed no additional legislation to secure the results originally intended.

CHAPTER XVII.
HOMEWARD BOUND.

ALL hands were called on the morning of the 27th at 4 o'clock, and, an hour later, we had picked up anchor and were steaming away, bound for New York. We found the weather extremely rough in the vicinity of Hatteras, and during three or four days, with a terrific gale blowing in our teeth, occasionally blinding sheets of rain and a heavy choppy sea, we were enabled to make but little headway. On the 6th of December she was pitching and tossing as though the very masts would be sprung, and nothing in sight save great angry waves surging and rolling with the noise of thunder, and overhead a sky of inky darkness. The captain sent her off with the wind during the afternoon under close-reefed topsails, whereby she was considerably eased, and towards evening of the next day the storm had greatly abated and she was gradually brought up to the course. For several days we had felt it growing steadily colder, and soon found it necessary to discard the thin apparel which had been so long essential, for heavier and more seasonable clothing. On the morning of the 8th the sun came up bright and clear, the darkness and storm of the preceding days had been succeeded by blue skies, and a sea throughout whose wide expanse the waters rose and fell in regular, peaceful motion.

The spirits of officers and crew were not less buoyant than the noble ship, which had voyaged so successfully over thousands of miles, until now our destined port is, at best, but a few hours off. Cape Henry "Light" was sighted shortly before midnight, all hands having patiently remained on deck to catch a view of the first landmark to be seen along the coast.

At midnight of the 9th we came abreast of the Cape May lightship; a few hours later Barnegat "Light" was made, while other familiar scenery along the route became more and more indistinct beneath the sombre shadows of approaching night.

On the 10th of December we steamed with flying colors up the bay, and refreshed our vision with the sights thought, dreamed, and talked of for many months; a little later the towering domes and steeples of the great metropolis, and the unequalled combination of strength and beauty which spans East River, the Brooklyn bridge; and at 10.30 the *Juniata* dropped anchor in Raritan Bay.

The transfer of prisoners and invalids was made during the afternoon, and the next day the customs officers paid the ship a visit, which occasioned considerable excitement, especially among the men, most of whom decided to relinquish their little store of foreign goods rather than diminish the size of their pay-day stock by giving up the duty.

After inspecting the numerous boxes, packages, and bundles of every description strewn over the deck belonging to the men, it was decided, much to their relief, to pass them free. The officers did not come off so well, and were obliged to pay for the privilege of showing a great variety of beautiful and curious articles to their friends.

The captain was ordered to Washington by telegram on the 14th, and returned next night. The final inspection took place on the 16th and 17th, and on the representation of the board it was decided that the *Juniata* should not be put out of commission, but refitted and a new crew sent to her.

On the afternoon of the 19th we got under way, landed the ship's ammunition at the magazine, and then proceeded to the Navy Yard.

Wednesday, the 23d of December, was red-letter day — the crew were to receive their money and final liberty. It was not strange, therefore, in view of this long-anticipated event, that all hands were the least bit restless the preceding night — indeed, many of the boys turned out as early as three A. M., and cooled their throbbing temples in the crisp December breeze.

At 9.30 the exciting operation began, the men filing through the cabin to receive their money from the paymaster and discharges from the captain, and a few hours later it would have required the entire able force of Inspector Byrnes to rally a corporal's guard.

The captain handed me my discharge (which suggests that your voyage is also at an end, fellow traveler,) on the afternoon of the 24th, and thereby intimated that the late cabin-boy of the *Juniata* would not be expected on the morrow at the Christmas dinner of Uncle Sam.

THE END.

www.ingramcontent.com/pod-product-compliance
Lightning Source LLC
Chambersburg PA
CBHW031904220426
43663CB00006B/753